DESIGN OUTDOORS

Inspiring everyone to grow

DESIGN OUTDOORS

Projects and plans for a stylish garden

Matt Keightley

Photography by Marianne Majerus

Contributing Editor Tiffany Daneff

MITCHELL BEAZLEY

CONTENTS

Introduction

MATT KEIGHTLEY

I have been designing gardens for close on two decades and still get that same rush of excitement and wave of energy when I put pen to paper for the first time for a project. It's an incredible thrill, planning a space and transforming the way clients both visualise and use their own properties in ways they never thought possible.

I have selected 35 beautiful gardens, some my own work, others created by many of the leading designers working today, and explored their key features, design details, material selection, planting choices and design principles. A handful of the gardens have been created for the internationally celebrated RHS Chelsea Flower Show; the rest are 'real' gardens in a variety of locations – from the heart of the city to the wilds of the country. The gardens have been chosen to provide a diverse collection of contemporary styled spaces, ranging from minimalist to family-friendly. There will be something to learn and something to take home, and you will finish the book feeling motivated to make the small alterations necessary in order to turn your good garden into a great one.

Through the remarkable photography of Marianne Majerus, I will take you behind the eyes of the designer in a way that deconstructs the elements of each garden, enabling you to see clearly why and how they work so effectively. Annotated plans created by the designer of each garden will help you to interpret the gardens and put the photographs in context, and allow you to see how each designer has started the design process and established the most appropriate way forward for that specific space.

Admittedly, it can be daunting and often tricky to know where to start when redesigning an outdoor space, especially if, like many of the people I meet, you enjoy spending time

> ## A beautiful garden should be regarded as an additional room that is just as important as your other living spaces.

in your garden but cannot envisage its potential, beyond the existing obligatory patio at the back of the house – rammed to the edges with furniture, toys and failing pot plants. So, whether you are looking to completely redesign your garden or just rejuvenate a few features, or are simply seeking some inspiration, this book is full of incredible ideas, tips and advice that will leave you desperate to improve and care more for your garden.

Rather than an uninspired garden that you only use when you feel compelled to because the sun decides to come out, your precious outdoor commodity should be integral to the planning of your home. Your garden is essentially an additional room that is just as important as the other living spaces in your home, and this book will provide you with the visual inspiration and experienced know-how to help you transform it into an outdoor space like no other.

Opposite: Standing proudly in the RHS 'Feel Good Garden' (see pp18–25), designed for the 2018 RHS Chelsea Flower Show. The space showed the ways in which gardens can be used to improve physical health and psychological wellbeing, encouraging users to interact with the garden by following the meandering paths to enjoy the textural planting.

The Wider Landscape

Cleverly linking a garden with the wider landscape has a variety of benefits.

1. Create a sense of depth and a feeling of space by blending your garden into the landscape beyond its boundary. You can prevent abrupt stops around your border by planting in front of fences and walls, helping to disguise where your space ends and the adjoining space begins.

2. Tree choice and placement can play a huge part in 'borrowing' the wider landscape. Look at existing species nearby. If you think they will work in your own garden, plant some to gain immediate continuity.

3. Use overhanging branches from a neighbour's garden to your advantage; they can often be used to frame views, soften pergolas, give privacy and provide frames for birdfeeders.

4. Leading the eye to the surrounding landscape lengthens views and creates the illusion of a larger space. Think how you want the garden to be appreciated horizontally and vertically. For example, softer planting in the foreground with a bold feature at the rear will direct the focus of the viewer.

5. Create an exaggerated sense of perspective by exploiting a particular feature in the landscape. This might be a beautiful building or specimen tree. Build drama into your space and gradually draw people's attention through the garden with changing planting levels before finally focusing on a distinctive object in the distance beyond your boundary.

6. The height of nearby trees can be used to create a greater sense of space. Try graduating the level of the planting, from ground-level plants through medium shrubs, tall grasses and, finally, medium trees. This makes for a more natural transition between the garden and the wider landscape.

7. Monitoring how the sun tracks round your garden, and thus where neighbours' trees are likely to cast shade, will help you plan the layout and design more thoroughly.

Balance

Create synergy and continuity
throughout your garden.

1. The balance between hard and soft landscaping is the most important and arguably the trickiest to get right. Put simply, contemporary and minimalist designs have a higher proportion of hard landscaping to planting than classical ones (although they also need to suit the aspect and wider landscape).

2. Take advantage of level changes when balancing a space. They create depth in smaller gardens and a larger surface area to work with. If you need to step down into the garden, add drama by creating a space that requires steps back up to the level of the internal floor.

3. Using colour to balance a garden is fun. Not only will the space look 'right' if colour is used consistently, but you can also manipulate the way people view it. Once the structural planting is established, drift colours from one side of the garden to the other, providing balance across the width and a rhythm throughout the scheme.

4. Selecting the right materials ensures balance and synergy with the interior. Noting a client's preferences in interior finishes and accessories helps create a balanced feel between the two spaces.

5. Textural balance can create depth, layers and perspective. Try grasses and perennials in the foreground with some topiary peeping out behind them. This is more intriguing and satisfying to look at than if they are the other way round.

6. Planning a garden proportionally is vital for balance. For example, try using multiple seating areas to stop a terrace dominating the scheme and so create a more aesthetically pleasing space.

7. Aim to balance 'mass and void' (busy space versus open ground). In formal schemes, create symmetry from left to right – trees on either side can frame views into a void, giving the garden a sense of place. In an area beyond or around the void (lawn, gravel or a terrace), use mid-height shrubs to add movement around the blank space.

Opposite: A contemporary Corten steel retaining wall cuts through this naturalistic planting scheme, accenting the shapes and forms beyond the garden.
Above: The beautiful natural texture and vibrant green fronds of *Dicksonia antarctica* (soft tree fern) contrast with the muted tones of the streetscape.
Right: The warm, honey tones of the timber walkway are picked up in the subtle flecks of orange through the planting, marrying hard and soft.

Water

Water can transform
the atmosphere of a space
in a variety of ways.

---

1. Use the sound of running water to enhance the atmosphere of a space. In urban environments, mask traffic noise by increasing the scale of the drop from water source to reservoir.

2. Use vertical planes for the movement of water. It draws attention immediately, as you often see the water feature as soon as you enter a garden. It is also a good use of space in smaller gardens, as you can recirculate the water using a compact reservoir.

3. Water control is important. Both the level and the clarity of the water make a huge difference to the end result. Position the balance tank and controls away from the main garden or in a nearby shed for easy inspection so that they do not affect the aesthetics of the garden.

4. A perfectly still body of water is a great way to create reflections of the surrounding garden or of a feature such as a tree or sculpture. This can work in both open ground and a slightly more enclosed environment. Either way, circulate the water when you can to prevent stagnation.

5. If you have room, a rill can be an effective way to guide people through a space. You need a simple recirculating system and then gravity takes care of the movement of the water through the rill itself. Adjust the turbulence through the material you use and design a shallow, yet broad, profile so that children can enjoy the water too.

6. Lighting water can transform the look and atmosphere of the space. Be sure to make the fittings as discreet as possible to avoid glare or reflection of the individual LEDs. It is not always necessary to use underwater fittings; if you uplight nearby trees or features they will reflect beautifully on the water's surface.

7. Water can be used as a key feature of the garden design to draw immediate attention, or it can be a subtle addition that needs to be discovered, creating mystery and intrigue. Consider carefully how water could best fit into your space.

Lighting

A carefully considered lighting scheme will turn a good garden into a great garden.

1. Good lighting is more about the effect than the look of the fitting. Where possible, try to hide light fittings behind benches and among foliage. Always purchase good-quality fittings to ensure longevity, but also consistency around the scheme.

2. Less is more when it comes to wattage. You have more control over the effect or scene if you stick to low-level lights. Rather than using a 12-watt floodlight bulb, try four 3-watt spikes so you can control the beam angles and illuminate exactly what you want.

3. Practical path and step lights do not need to look utilitarian. Consider the fixing detail and how the fitting can be positioned discreetly. The effect should add to the wider lighting scheme and not look like a runway to a fire exit. Low-level strip lighting works extremely well.

4. If there are trees or shrubs close enough to a path, try uplighting them and you will get the best of both worlds; the tree will look fantastic and the path will be illuminated.

5. Individual light controls are key to creating the right lighting atmosphere for different events. I prefer to use multiple switches or programmed scenes, rather than a single switch for the entire scheme. This approach enables you to manipulate how you view and use the space.

6. Avoid colour-changing lights. Cool to warm white is all you need to create a romantic or atmospheric space. Seek professional advice on the kelvin (colour temperature) required. I usually opt for 2700–3000K, which is warmer than daylight and a good all-rounder for most gardens.

7. Enhance your lighting scheme by adding candles. Lanterns or tealights add the finishing touches that turn a beautiful garden into a magical one.

8. Avoid glare at all costs. If a guest walks into your garden and stares directly into a lamp, it will ruin the experience. Consider the beam angles and fitting positions to ensure you don't walk around your garden squinting.

Opposite left: Shards of steel erupt from the planting at different heights as water courses out of each of them, providing turbulence in the pond below.
Opposite right: The brimming water in these Corten steel troughs reflects the surrounding garden.
Above: Discreet lighting can draw focus to simplistic planting.
Right: Hidden uplighting creates a beautifully warm glow around the base of this Japanese maple.

Outdoor Living

The position of a seating area can change the way you move through and use your garden.

1. A recent movement towards expansive glass façades on our homes has implications for the way we design our urban residential landscapes. It is more important than ever to create synergy between interior and exterior spaces. Make an additional outdoor room by using accent themes, colours and styles from the interior.

2. Creating multiple seating areas is a great way to encourage more frequent use of a garden. A border at the back of the garden may look beautiful, but you are more likely to visit if there is a bench nearby.

3. Installing fire in some form is a great way to encourage you to enjoy your garden during the colder months. Fire features range from very basic fire baskets to bio-fuel tables and bespoke purpose-built fire walls.

4. Outdoor cooking is a hugely sociable activity in the garden if you position the cooking area correctly. Opt for a traditional approach using good-quality equipment (with charcoal/lumpwood) rather than a fancy-looking outdoor kitchen that uses gas.

5. Enclosure can provide a heightened sense of intimacy, privacy and seclusion. There are many effective structures and planting choices that can help to envelop a secluded spot. Try open roof structures for growing plants and opening up views of the sky.

6. Bespoke furniture is often the best solution for a small space. It can be tucked into just about any corner and planters can also be incorporated to add interest. Before ordering expensive materials, create a plywood tester to check proportions – the seat pad of a lounge chair, for example, should be 42cm (17in) high with a back at an 18-degree angle!

7. Pots and planters often provide the finishing touches to a garden design. These seemingly unimportant accessories can transform a nice-looking garden into a carefully considered and truly bespoke space.

8. It is worth including storage in your garden to tuck away tools, children's toys and cushions in winter. I prefer to design bespoke sheds or storage units to ensure they are as discreet as possible, tucked in behind planting and often painted dark green so they blend in and are unobtrusive.

Opposite left: This open pavilion, which offers both shade and sanctuary, is as beautiful as it is practical.
Opposite right: Cleverly integrated within the scheme, this outdoor shower simulates a monsoon and works perfectly with the style of planting.
Below: Single-species planting in this understated yet striking garden accents the hard landscaping.
Right: A seamless transition between material interfaces gives a sense of calm.

Less is More

It is often harder to work with a restricted or minimalist palette, but if the design is executed correctly, it can result in a garden that feels effortless.

1. A restrained planting palette is bold, exciting and, if meticulously planned, can produce a uniquely confident design. Use evergreen shrubs to provide backbone and structure, but remember that undulation and movement are also crucial. Choose a colour palette and limit the number of perennial species, simply increasing the quantity of each for a mind-blowing effect.

2. Specimen trees can add all the interest and drama you need. Visit a few nurseries once you know the species you need and treat your choice as if you were selecting a piece of art. Each and every part of the tree needs to be perfect for a restrained space.

3. Constancy of tone is important, so if you decide to use multiple materials you need to be sure that the tones are cohesive and do not clash with one another. Samples and mood boards are helpful at the design stage to establish the final feeling and detailing.

4. 'Less is more' doesn't always refer to the number of materials you use. Some gardens benefit from a single choice, while others are just as effective if multiple materials are used – this introduces subtle texture, which can bring a change in pace and rhythm.

5. Detail is key to creating something truly effortless in appearance and incredibly relaxing in experience. Consider how material interfaces are treated; every detail should feel deliberate, seamless and 'just so'.

6. Don't worry about leaving blank or open spaces in the garden. Just as the white space in a drawing can create as much intrigue as the detailed sketch, so open areas in a garden can be restful. These areas provide space for quiet contemplation and reduce unnecessary intensity and complexity.

7. Consider furniture in a similar way to sculpture in terms of its synergy with the garden. It should look well positioned, without dominating an area, and should be integral to the scheme. Ensure the material choices complement the hard landscaping and flow into the planting.

8. The layout of the garden should be as uncomplicated as the palette of plants and materials. Regardless of the level changes, visitors should feel they can move around the space with ease.

The Great Outdoors

You can encourage children to enjoy the garden even within the confines of the city.

1. Dens can keep children busy for hours each weekend. Something as simple as the canopy of a tree or the cover of a hedgerow can bring a great deal of pleasure. Create the space with planting rather than a plastic structure, which can ruin the look of the garden.

2. Create a mud kitchen where children can get their hands dirty. So as not to sacrifice too much space in the garden, I encourage my children to use a large terracotta pot instead; they enjoy emptying and refilling it with mud, digging for worms, collecting stones and making mud pies.

3. Encourage children to learn more about nature by adding bird feeders and bug boxes, and including plants that attract pollinators. Not only will this entice wildlife, but it will encourage children to engage with the garden.

4. Space to grow your own fruit and veg is a must, even in the smallest of gardens. Help your children learn more about where food comes from by involving them. It is so satisfying to find inches of growth on your runner beans each morning!

5. The act of gardening is enough to excite children and they love the great outdoors as a result. If you encourage your kids they will soon be out in the garden every weekend in their oversized gloves weeding, collecting snails and covering the paving in chalk art reminiscent of cave paintings.

6. Watering is something you can do as a family and this important task becomes a fun challenge for children. Don't forget to recycle all the paddling pool water at the end of the day by using it to water containers.

7. Try to minimise the number of toys in the garden – there is more than enough for children to play with outdoors if they use their imagination. If you must have toys – and we all have a sandpit and a few bright plastic items – find a spot in which they can be stored out of sight when the children aren't in the garden.

8. Children love to explore, so creating secret paths and hideaways is a great way to encourage them to use the garden.

Opposite left: Natural material is used in an ingenious way to create steps that are sculptural in their own right.

Opposite right: A trampoline has been recessed into the ground to prevent an unsightly frame spoiling the scheme.

Left: Visually and aromatically stunning, the planting in this garden encourages engagement.

Below: The planting in this scheme is so elegant and inviting that you can't help but want to enter the space.

The Senses

Stimulate the senses in the garden using fragrant plants, interesting sounds and striking colours and textures.

1. To create a truly immersive garden, provoke engagement and interaction through the tactile nature of the elements you choose, whether this is the crunch of gravel underfoot, the feeling of grasses running through your fingers or the ergonomic pleasures of furniture. Try combining hard and soft landscaping – hard granite juxtaposed with soft grasses is a good example from my 2014 RHS Chelsea Flower Show garden (see pp166–173). Play on the senses with your garden and you will create something unforgettable.

2. Visual stimulation can come in many different forms and work across all styles of garden. Aim to create something striking and memorable. This does not have to be a single focal point or sculpture. Instead, consider how the garden is put together to create a comfortable and cohesive environment.

3. Colour is a superb way to set the tone and evoke emotion. A cool, muted palette is often associated with a relaxing space, but there are other options. Yellow, for example, is uplifting, while bold colour contrasts can be exciting and add to the experience.

4. There is nothing better to stimulate the senses than a herb garden, as herbs have fantastic aromas. You don't need a lot of space, as they can easily be grown in pots. Herbs also look great in a perennial scheme.

5. Fragrant areas can be achieved with the right planting and enhanced with clever positioning. Plant everyday herbs around path fringes, so the aromas are released as you brush past.

6. Sound outdoors can be a source of relaxation. There is nothing like the gentle trickle of moving water. It is mesmerising and therapeutic – just the qualities you need to stimulate the senses and reduce stress.

1

Show Stoppers

CASE STUDY

A Feel-good Garden

MATT KEIGHTLEY

Intense and immersive, this RHS Chelsea Flower Show 2017 garden heightens the senses and lures you in. The balance is carefully considered to ensure there is an abundance of detail to admire without this being forced. There is a natural flow throughout, which is helped by the inclusion of water. Areas of planting that build intensively are pacified by the flanking body of water and also the sound of gentle turbulence where the water wall meets the rill.

An unusual and effective use of *Pinus mugo* (dwarf mountain pine) cultivars en masse creates undulation and movement through the planting. Glaucous tones and tight shapes provide a perfect backbone for the entire scheme. Elegant hues of cream and rusty reds drift through and project above the grasses; these act like a glue in the garden – they are not the main focus, but are nonetheless integral to the planting.

Pushing and pulling levels and manipulating the perspective has resulted in a 10 × 10m (33 × 33ft) plot that feels much larger than it actually is. A gently tapering path immediately gives the garden an enhanced sense of depth. The sculptural wall at the rear draws you in and encourages you to engage, while moss panels provide a striking break from the concrete-like facets as well as a link to the shade-loving planting growing at its feet.

On passing the sculptural back wall, the boundary slips into a smooth radius that invites users to follow it round and down the steps into a secluded seating area. Changing levels and dropping into this space really connects you to the garden – even the pebble seats are incredibly satisfying to touch.

Right: This tactile garden features geometric forms juxtaposed with a soft planting palette. Angular pathways glide across water, while rocks offer a place for contemplation. Pines, grasses, ferns and mosses blend in this relaxing space.

A FEEL-GOOD GARDEN

Design Checklist

1. Consider perspective, especially in smaller garden schemes. A tapered path creates a visual illusion, making a garden feel longer and giving a greater sense of space.

2. Change levels to dramatically transform the atmosphere of a garden. Drops in level can simultaneously create intrigue and a secluded, intimate socializing space. Using vertical elements and planting your boundaries are very effective ways to draw in the wider landscape.

3. Strike a balance between the elements of hard and soft landscaping to put people at ease. This balance can tip either way depending on the aspect, style and size of the space, and also sometimes the budget. Try to reduce imposing 'moments' by breaking up hard-material interfaces – for example, areas of paving that meet a wall can be softened with planting.

4. Use standard materials creatively for a truly bespoke space. Stone can be used in large format, finished with varying textures and colour-enhanced to bring out its rich natural tones. Even the choice of paving joint can be used to manipulate the way people travel around a garden.

5. Water movement has therapeutic qualities. Introducing a gentle flow and the sound of trickling water can help people enjoy a space, distracting them and reducing stress and anxiety.

6. Enrapture people with your use of texture. Foliage and form can make a bold statement in a garden and establish the structure throughout. Pair hard foliage with light grasses and perennials to achieve a satisfying and immersive composition.

7. Choose a restrained colour palette for greater sophistication. In this garden, I used deep, musky reds and creams, knowing that the colours would pop against the glaucous tones of the pines. To create maximum effect, consider what the perennial colours will be sitting in front of.

8. Use furniture as sculpture by integrating it seamlessly into the rest of the design scheme. Pieces such as the pebbles used in this design provoke interaction as a result of their tactile nature and therefore enhance the user's experience.

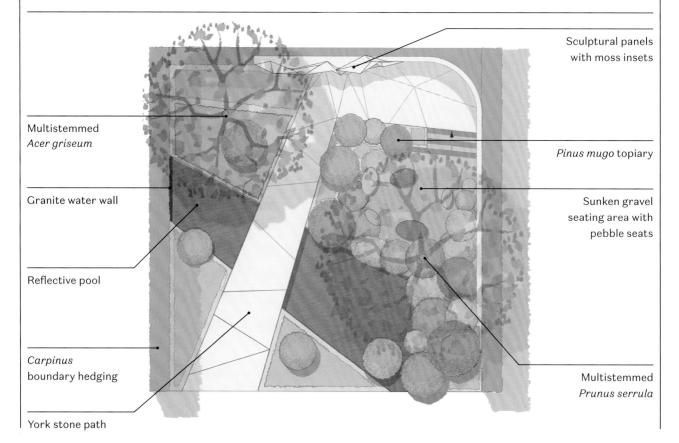

Multistemmed *Acer griseum*

Granite water wall

Reflective pool

Carpinus boundary hedging

York stone path

Sculptural panels with moss insets

Pinus mugo topiary

Sunken gravel seating area with pebble seats

Multistemmed *Prunus serrula*

A FEEL-GOOD GARDEN

The
Details

A sheet of granite subtly carved with geometric shapes creates subtle water movement and provides the perfect backdrop for the glowing leaves of an *Acer griseum* (paperbark maple).

An exciting mix of punchy and texturally striking, partial shade-loving plants. Crimson tones draw the focus, while darker foliage gives the bed layers and a sense of depth.

The beautifully rich tones of *Iris* 'Kent Pride', a tall bearded iris, punctuate an otherwise muted, soft and elegant planting scheme.

Discreet light fittings bring the garden to life by night. Uplighting the *Prunus serrula* (Tibetan cherry) casts mesmerising shadows on the nearby wall while highlighting the beautiful, almost metallic bark.

Uplighting casts fascinating shadows across the facets of the boundary wall and provides a glow at the foot of the *Acer griseum* (paperbark maple).

The stems of *Prunus serrula* (Tibetan cherry), with their flaking bark glistening in the sunlight, emerge from an underplanting of *Pinus mugo* (dwarf mountain pine).

Tumbled stone lines the pools of water, providing a dark backdrop for the fringe of planting that surrounds them.

Hidden Oasis

CHARLOTTE ROWE

This particular space contains an incredibly long path – 20m (66ft) in total – with boundary walls on each side leading to a very irregularly shaped main garden that is surrounded by seven different neighbouring gardens.

Indeed, the path into the garden from the house was so long that the owners didn't really use the garden as much as they wanted. Now, though, visitors cannot wait to set off down the pretty gravel path that leads towards the giant firepit and beyond to the oval lawn. Nowhere is there any hint of the surrounding gardens, which are now hidden behind planted fencing and trellis, while mature trees complete the deceit.

As soon as you step out of the house there's a raised breakfast area with comfortable two-seater sofas from where you can look over the pale limestone paving and steps, which are punctuated with seemingly natural mounds of greenery, and on through tumbling rose arches. To the left, a row of pleached *Carpinus* (hornbeam) helps lead the eye to another arch and beyond to the L-shaped limestone bench. This abuts the elliptical lawn at the heart of the garden.

The boundary walls are traditional London stock brick. These work well with both the pale limestone and the dark grey slatted fence, which will one day disappear completely behind climbers. Loose informal planting softens the hard edges, while evergreen globes in a variety of sizes bring the whole design together.

Left: The space's most tricky area has been transformed into its star feature – a narrow corridor garden of pale stone and gravel that billows with soft green foliage, leading the eye from the house to the firepit and the oval lawn.

HIDDEN OASIS

Design Checklist

1. Choose the largest firepit you can to create sculptural impact. Firepits come in all shapes and sizes, and to suit every budget and style of garden.

2. Soften hard edges with plants, whether this is on paths, up walls or over trellis arches. Here, roses have been trained up trellis to create arches over the long path. The acid-yellows of euphorbia work well to light up the shade under the trees.

3. Prune the lower branches of trees and shrubs to allow more light to reach the ground below, enabling shade- and drought-tolerant plants to thrive. This treatment also gives a pleasing shape to a tree's trunk.

4. Use a range of shrubs and small specimen trees to provide mixed-height plantings and a planterly effect. *Hydrangea arborescens* 'Annabelle', *Sarcoccoca confusa* (sweet box), *Hebe parviflora* var. *angustifolia* and *Hydrangea quercifolia* all work well in a shady town garden.

5. Invest in rusted iron plant supports. These come in a variety of shapes and sizes; here they are used for growing *Lathyrus odoratus* (sweet pea) in summer but they look great all year round as they provide upright structure and natural colour.

6. Create a loose contemporary effect by planting perennials such as *Gaura, Helleborus, Alchemilla, Sedum, Knautia, Salvia* and *Digitalis* (foxglove) so that they flow through grasses like *Stipa* and *Molinia*.

7. Plant paving and gravel areas with low-growing, mounding plants such as *Galium, Vinca* and thyme, which give off a lovely scent when walked on, especially at night.

8. Consider the garden at night. Here, subtle lighting is positioned to illuminate flower beds and specimen trees, as well as to highlight focal points such as the rose arches and the seat beside the firepit.

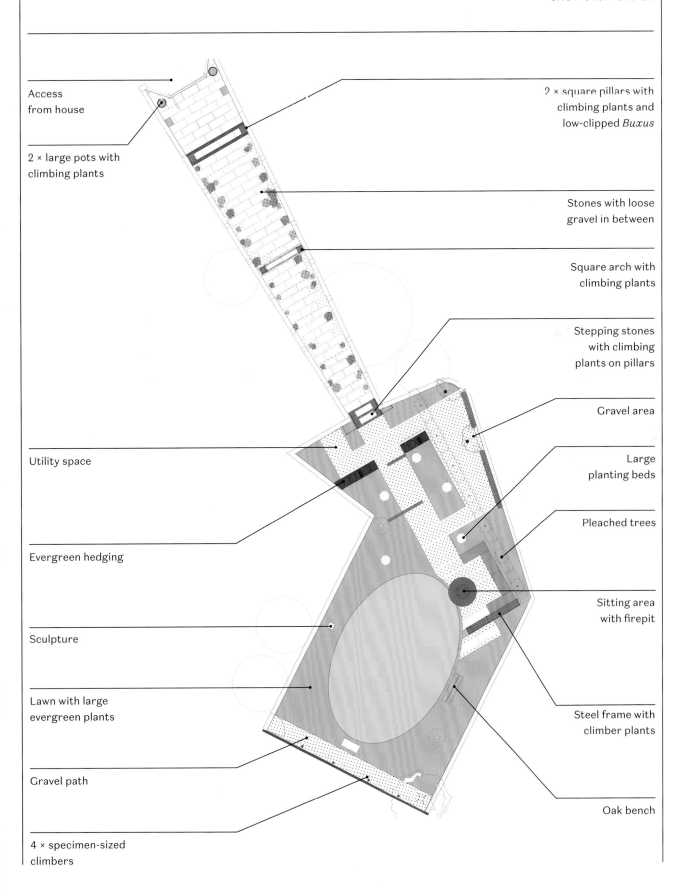

Access
from house

2 × large pots with
climbing plants

Utility space

Evergreen hedging

Sculpture

Lawn with large
evergreen plants

Gravel path

4 × specimen-sized
climbers

2 × square pillars with
climbing plants and
low-clipped *Buxus*

Stones with loose
gravel in between

Square arch with
climbing plants

Stepping stones
with climbing
plants on pillars

Gravel area

Large
planting beds

Pleached trees

Sitting area
with firepit

Steel frame with
climber plants

Oak bench

Irregularly positioned, narrow strips of groundcover plants and stone add interest to the gravel path.

Stone paviours laid crossways create width. Shade- and drought-tolerant plants grow in the gravel on each side.

A mixed spring planting of *Tulipa* 'Queen of Night', acid-green euphorbia and aquilegias with a backdrop of clematis climbing on trellis, which is painted to match the new fencing.

Neatly clipped *Buxus sempervirens* balls (common box) frame the oak seat, which is sited to afford views across the lawn.

Contemporary grey-painted fencing 'disappears' behind *Trachelospermum jasminoides* (star jasmine).

Euphorbia characias subsp. *characias* 'Humpty Dumpty' and *Allium* 'Mount Everest' are planted at the foot of a row of uplit pleached *Carpinus betulus.*

The firepit with an underlit
limestone bench.

The Details

Lanterns flank a matching pair of sofas
made from stainless steel and Batyline
fabric to create clean modern lines.

CASE STUDY

Low Maintenance

TONY WOODS

Is it possible to create a beautiful garden that is also low-maintenance? This is a question that garden designers are asked all the time. Here, Tony Woods has worked magic by turning what was a depressingly muddy lawn with narrow side beds and little else into a fabulously chic back garden. Better still, the new garden does not take a lot to keep it looking this good. So how did he do it? First, Tony built a small limestone dining terrace and outdoor kitchen close to the house and another more relaxed area on a raised deck at the back underneath the existing mature cherry tree. A rusted Corten steel fireplace was set into what was once a white freestanding wall that hid a garden shed. Painting the wall dark grey gives it the look of an expensive render. Panels of horizontal fence run down both side walls, in front of which multistemmed and fragrant olive trees are planted at intervals. A couple more olives stand at the edge of the deck, framed in low box squares and uplit at night, creating sculptural forms with their elegant stems.

The borders were widened and the heavy clay London soil improved with imported topsoil and well-rotted manure before being planted with easy-to-look-after hydrangeas, *Anemone × hybrida* (Japanese anemone) and *Hakonechloa macra* (Japanese forest grass). *Trachelospermum jasminoides* (star jasmine) is being trained up the fence. The *pièce de résistance* – and one that the clients were most worried about – is the artificial lawn. Despite their fears, this has perhaps proved the most successful innovation. It stays fresh, clean and green, needs little maintenance and has put off local foxes.

Right: Teak sofas sit on the hardwood deck and a steel fireplace has been set into the original freestanding wall. Good-quality artificial turf has transformed a persistently muddy lawn and given the garden a new lease of life.

LOW MAINTENANCE

Design Checklist

1. Choose low-maintenance limestone paving. A good alternative to the Egyptian limestone used here is Jura Beige limestone, which is suitable for contemporary gardens as well as more traditional surroundings.

2. Opt for artificial grass. This has improved greatly, especially the elite ranges. It is easy to install and maintain, simply requiring brushing to remove leaves and debris. It is ideal for low-maintenance gardening and areas where real grass lawns will not thrive.

3. Go for contemporary fencing. Western cedar slatted screen fence panels weather to a silvery grey. Horizontal fencing looks smarter and more contemporary than vertical timbers. Panels can be bought in varying lengths and with a kit that contains the necessary battens, posts and nails.

4. Consider an alternative to box. *Buxus* can be completely defoliated by box tree caterpillars, the caterpillars of the Asian *Cydalima perspectalis* moth. Consider evergreen alternatives such as berberis, *Ilex crenata* (box-leaved holly) or *Taxus* (yew).

5. Satisfy the senses. The fragrant or sweet olive, *Osmanthus fragrans*, has scented flowers in summer and leathery evergreen leaves that make it an ideal wall or hedging plant. Multistemmed trees should be planted 1.2–2m (4–6½ft) apart. Flowers form on old wood, so pruning will reduce blooms.

6. Make low-maintenance borders high on impact. To achieve punch, choose a few plants with strong contrasting forms and repeat them throughout the design. Here, *Anemone hortensis* (broad-leaved anemones) contrast with bladed *Hakonechloa macra* (Japanese forest grass) and the white spherical blooms of hydrangea.

7. Add a contemporary feel to your garden. Bamboo lanterns work really well here, as the orange candle sits beautifully against the dark grey painted wall, echoing the flames in the fireplace. Choose a lantern with a glass insert so that the wind does not blow out the flame every five minutes – or singe the bamboo.

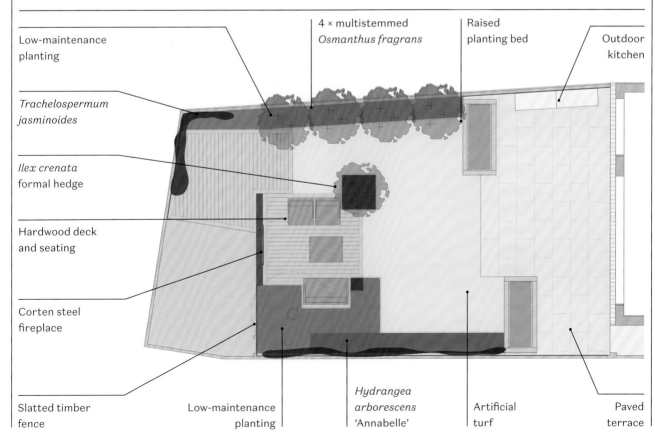

Low-maintenance planting

Trachelospermum jasminoides

Ilex crenata formal hedge

Hardwood deck and seating

Corten steel fireplace

Slatted timber fence

4 × multistemmed *Osmanthus fragrans*

Raised planting bed

Outdoor kitchen

Low-maintenance planting

Hydrangea arborescens 'Annabelle'

Artificial turf

Paved terrace

The table on the limestone dining terrace with multistemmed *Osmanthus fragrans* (fragrant olive) growing against the fence.

A bamboo lantern with an orange candle hanging in the existing mature cherry tree.

Hydrangea arborescens 'Annabelle' is planted with fragrant *Trachelospermum jasminoides* (star jasmine) scrambling along the fence behind.

Double-direction wall lights on the fence provide a gentle diffused light above and below.

The Details

Euphorbia with a planting of variegated miscanthus behind.

Hakonechloa macra (Japanese forest grass) and *Anemone × hybrida* 'Honorine Jobert' under the *Osmanthus fragrans* at the edge of the artificial lawn.

CASE STUDY

Rooftop Paradise

CHRISTOPHER BRADLEY-HOLE

Who would expect to find irises and pine trees flourishing on a city-centre roof garden? The skill in this design lies in creating a garden that seems to defy all the restrictions placed upon it. It shows that you can have bold colour, trees and a collection of heritage plants within a minimal, perfectly proportioned, contemporary setting. Roofs are exposed places and require careful planning to avoid overloading the support structure. Here, timber decking weathers to a soft grey, which subtly grounds the design and helps to set it in the surrounding roofscape. The existing wall was painted a rich sky-blue which provides a perfect background for the irises, as well as year-round colour. The zinc containers are light and manage to be both contemporary and traditional. Zinc is a perfect unifying material that offsets the darker green box and the light green spears of the iris leaves. Bearded irises come in a wealth of shades, from the softest whites through yellows, violets and rich reddish browns. They are show stoppers that appeal as much to everyday gardeners as collectors. There is a wide variety to choose from, which makes them an inspired idea for a roof garden. But perhaps the most dramatic flourish is provided by the living screen of *Pinus parviflora* (Japanese white pine), which gives this rooftop its distinctive allure.

Right: A screen of irises and pine trees sets this London roof garden apart. The blue wall provides a burst of colour all year round, as well as shelter from the elements. A small space like this needs sculptural furniture such as the aluminium table and chairs, which were designed by Jorge Pensi.

ROOFTOP PARADISE

Design Checklist

1. Consult an architect with experience in roof projects if you are planning any serious work. Not all roofs are strong enough to support large containers. Drainage can also be an issue. In some areas, you may require planning permission.

2. Install a timber deck on a flat roof to spread the weight. Timber decking weathers beautifully and is ideal for a rooftop as it can be floated above the drainage system. The spread of weight also allows you to use large containers, which are extremely heavy when saturated with water.

3. Select plants that are happy in exposed places. The conditions on a roof garden are not unlike those of coastal gardens, and plants will be buffeted by winds and in full sun. Dwarf bulbs and small, low-growing alpines have adapted to tolerate wind, as have plants that have needles (pines and grasses) or small leaves (cotoneaster).

4. Think about shelter. Box is useful as it provides year-round structure as well as shelter. You could also think about erecting a living screen of plants or trellis on which plants can be grown. Slatted screens are good because they allow the wind to filter through.

5. Lighten the load. Use lightweight soil and potting compost when planting up rooftop containers. Always make sure that pots contain drainage holes, or drill some if necessary, and use chunks of polystyrene at the bottom of pots to help drainage. Adding vermiculite to the planting medium will lighten it as well as improve drainage. Place heavy containers near load-bearing walls or over a load-bearing beam or joist.

6. Give container-grown plants extra attention. Raise pots off the ground so they don't become waterlogged and check that plant roots are not getting congested. Boost soil fertility by feeding container-grown plants regularly.

7. Install a watering system. Container-grown plants are thirsty and those on exposed roofs particularly so, both in winter and in summer because of the drying effect of the wind. The advice from the RHS is to water container-grown plants all year round except when it is freezing.

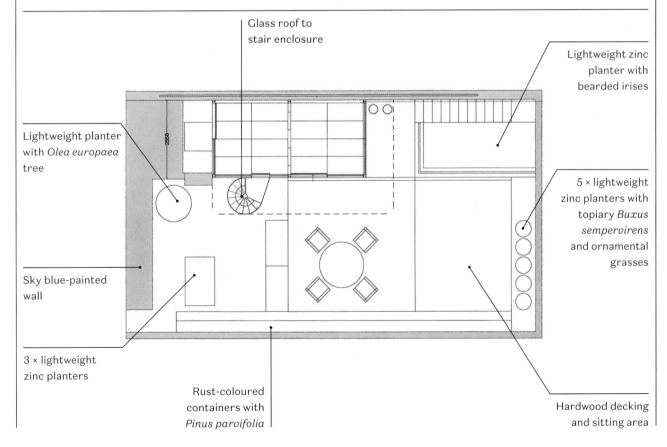

Glass roof to stair enclosure

Lightweight zinc planter with bearded irises

Lightweight planter with *Olea europaea* tree

5 × lightweight zinc planters with topiary *Buxus sempervirens* and ornamental grasses

Sky blue-painted wall

3 × lightweight zinc planters

Rust-coloured containers with *Pinus parvifolia*

Hardwood decking and sitting area

ROOFTOP PARADISE

The Details

Clipped *Buxus sempervirens*
(common box) and grasses in zinc
planters line the edge of the rooftop.

The tall, plum and burgundy bearded iris
'Indian Chief', with the lovely blue 'Chivalry',
a large ruffled iris.

The roof garden is edged with living screens of iris and pine.

Rust-coloured containers are planted with *Pinus parviflora* (Japanese white pine) to screen the garden from wind and sun. Their deep red tones echo the red-brick houses, as well as picking up the hues of *Iris* 'Indian Chief'.

Bearded irises in many hues, including bitone *Iris* 'Indian Chief', café-au-lait *Iris* 'Jean Cayeux', violet/ white *Iris* 'Whole Cloth' and blue *Iris* 'Chivalry'.

CASE STUDY

A Steeply Sloped Site

PETER BERG

This garden defies logic. It is just 20m (66ft) long, but the drop from the house level to the end of the plot is a huge 9m (30ft). The traditional design solution would be to create a series of steep terraces. Here, however, that would have resulted in vertiginous narrow 'steps', leaving no room to enjoy the space. Instead, the designer used cranes to lift basalt boulders into position to support the earthen banks and then placed further boulders and rocks so they seem to fall in a natural cascade down the slope. The basalt is interplanted with trees, shrubs and mixed perennials that look entirely natural. The result is an unforgettable garden that draws on the artistry of Japanese rock gardens with their characteristic tranquillity. Peter Berg learnt how to work with rocks by studying with Japanese masters. As Peter says, 'They have perfected the art of free stone placement. We developed the method so that the rocks could also be used to support construction.' A metal bridge reaches out into the space and extends the garden, which now feels full of optimism, as you can look across the landscape to a stream.

The plants were partly chosen to create natural-looking combinations that complement each other. More importantly for the long-term health of the plants (and ease of care for the owners), they were selected because they thrive in the conditions. Peter picks the trees and shrubs first, paying attention to form and character (again using a Japanese aesthetic). Next come the mixed perennials – the groundcover and flowering plants – and, finally, the grasses which knit the scheme together and move in the breeze.

Left: In the foreground, swaths of the white coneflower, *Echinacea purpurea* 'White Swan', are intermingled with grasses to flow down the slope and through the basalt rocks. From the bridge there's a view of a nearby stream.

A STEEPLY SLOPED SITE

Design Checklist

1. Fix the slope with rocks. Instead of building walls to hold back the earth, you can use large rocks to secure a steep terrain and prevent it from slipping. At the same time the rocks provide drama as well as paths to walk over and places to sit and ponder.

2. Make the most of views and surrounding features. Build a footbridge that overlooks a stream, as here, or open up the vista to expand the garden's horizons and take advantage of borrowed landscape.

3. Add a footbridge to bring form to a garden and overcome obstacles (such as the steep slope in this garden). Marry the style of bridge to that of the property and the planting to create a powerful statement. Hard forms can be softened with plants so that, over time, they appear as one.

4. Source local stone for a natural look that blends into the landscape. By using local materials you can blur the transition from the garden to the surrounding landscape. Sticking to the same stone for step plates, steps, grit and rocks creates a harmonious effect and brings the whole design together.

5. Use formal aluminium boxes as planters. Not only do they look great but, if they are set at the correct height, they can double up as seating. Better still, they can be used to hide and hold back the banked earth on a steep slope.

6. Use big plants for immediate effect. If you cannot wait for trees to grow and provide shade or privacy, buy large specimens. Many nurseries now specialize in supplying mature plants to create an 'instant' effect.

7. Select natural mixed perennials to create an organic landscape. The secret to success is to stick to a few varieties and plant them where they look at ease. Here, plants are tucked in between rocks and stones and flow as they do in nature.

8. Plant the right plant in the right place. To create a sustainable, low-maintenance and natural-looking garden, you need plants that thrive in your location. It never works trying to plant sun-lovers in shade or moisture-lovers in dry conditions. Work with your environment, not against it.

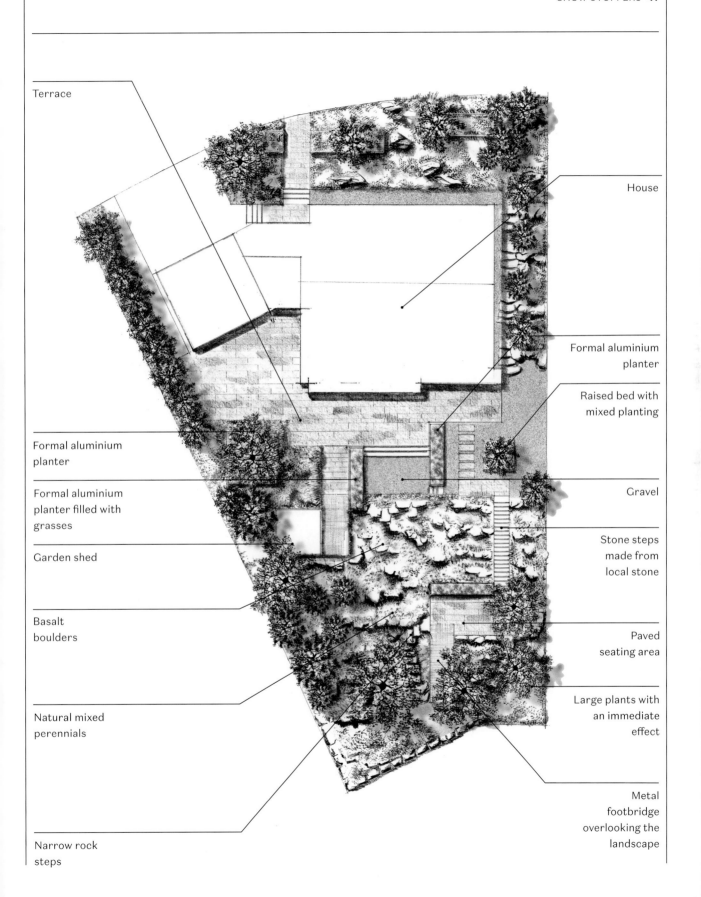

Terrace

House

Formal aluminium planter

Raised bed with mixed planting

Formal aluminium planter

Formal aluminium planter filled with grasses

Gravel

Garden shed

Stone steps made from local stone

Basalt boulders

Paved seating area

Natural mixed perennials

Large plants with an immediate effect

Metal footbridge overlooking the landscape

Narrow rock steps

The interplay of new planting and old trees integrates the second terrace with the garden.

Elegant grasses are planted to surround the rocks and create softly flowing movement.

The plants and the footbridge over the slope blur the boundary between the property and the nearby landscape.

From the footbridge, the nearby stream can be seen trickling beyond the garden's boundary.

Hakonechloa macra underneath an amelanchier, whose filigree foliage can be enjoyed from the kitchen window.

A STEEPLY SLOPED SITE

The Details

Formal and natural elements combine to create a path through the front garden.

The formal design of the upper terrace provides a thematic link to the modern house.

Basalt boulders and rocks have been naturalized by grasses and ferns.

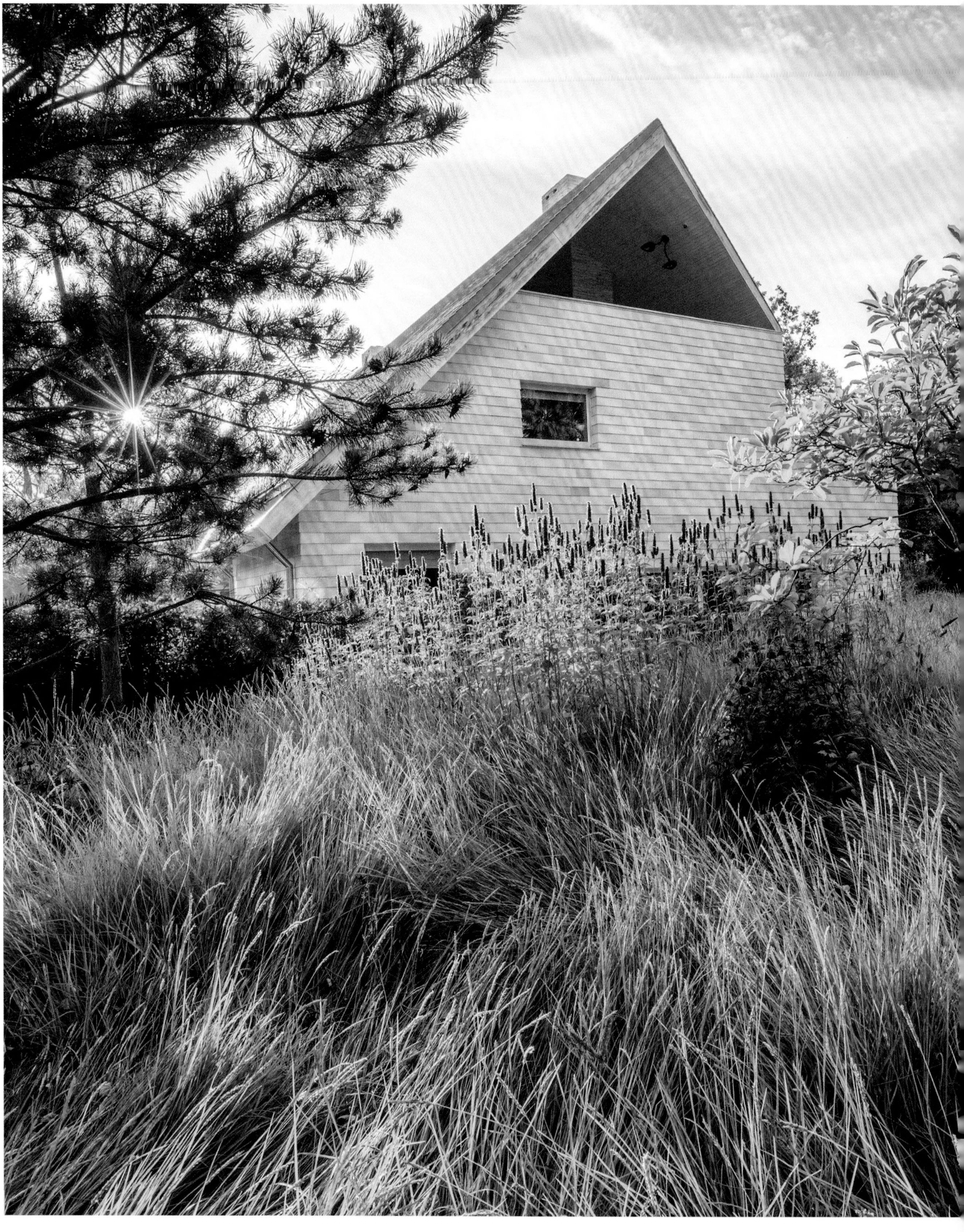

CASE STUDY

Natural Formality

CHRIS GHYSELEN & DOMINIQUE EEMAN

Robbrecht and Daem, the architects of this beautiful contemporary house, used the same white silver quartzite for the walls and all the hard landscaping, including the terraces and outdoor kitchen. The angular roof gives the building a strong sculptural shape. The owners wanted to balance this with an informal and colourful garden. Together Dominique Eeman, whose focus was on the overall design, and Chris Ghyselen, a keen plantsman, drew up a scheme that weaves together the lyrical wilderness of contemporary prairie planting with a more restrained evergreen woodland planting to provide colour from early spring to mid-autumn against a permanent green backdrop. The dramatic meadows of *Sesleria autumnalis* (autumn moor-grass) wave in the breeze and are interplanted with random drifts of flowering perennials that make these sweeping areas appear natural.

The house is about a mile from the coast and has some high ground and steep slopes, which had to be accommodated with steps, as well as a sloped and stepped lawn. These steep contours provide many and varied views. In places the poor soil had to be improved, but all the perennials are good garden plants that need the minimum of maintenance. Smaller trees such as *Cornus kousa* and magnolia are multistemmed, and provide a strong silhouette against the airy perennials. The indoor pool frames two views: one over a green slope, the other onto an outdoor shower. To the left stands a Japanese-style, cloud-pruned enkianthus, while the white flagstones are edged with ferns, *Asarum splendens* (Chinese wild ginger) and the blue star flowers of *Isotoma*.

Left: *Pinus sylvestris* and a *Magnolia crenata* stand tall in prairie beds of *Sesleria autumnalis* planted with drifts of tall purple *Agastache* 'Blackadder', *Echinacea purpurea* and pale lemon *Coreopsis verticillata* 'Moonbeam'.

NATURAL FORMALITY

Design Checklist

1. Unify the hard landscaping. The white silver quartzite used for the house and outdoor kitchen is continued through the terracing, steps and stepping stones to create a cool, minimalist design. This is repeated in the standing stones and the smooth, rounded boulders.

2. Plant naturalistic drifts of grasses to give the feel of the wild. This look works beautifully against the clean, minimal lines of contemporary architecture. *Sesleria autumnalis*, the perennial autumn moor-grass, grows to 60cm (24in) and is used both on the green roof and around the house.

3. Copy nature by growing perennials among the grasses. This technique is applied here using the white *Echinacea purpurea* 'Virgin', the deep purple, autumn-flowering spikes of *Agastache* 'Blackadder' and the lovely pale lemon tickseed, *Coreopsis verticillata* 'Moonbeam'. As a result of their random siting, these plants appear to have arrived by themselves.

4. Provide colour spots. Even a minimal naturalistic design of evergreens and grasses can provide highlights. Beside the steps, this is achieved through plantings of the red bistort, *Persicaria amplexicaulis* 'Firetail', yellow senecio and rich blue *Ceratostigma*. Near the steps are salvia, erigeron and the purple perennial wallflower, *Erysimum* 'Bowles's Mauve'.

5. Use a specimen tree as you would a sculpture. The cloud-pruned enkianthus in the basement shower area is placed by the floor-to-ceiling glass windows of the swimming pool, which frame it like a picture. In spring, it produces small, bell-shaped, creamy pink flowers, while autumn brings a fiery show of orange-red leaves.

6. Choose garden-worthy perennials for easier maintenance. The sloping border contains a dependable selection, including *Persicaria amplexicaulis* 'Firetail', *Amsonia tabernaemontana* var. *salicifolia* (eastern bluestar), *Anemone × hybrida* 'Königin Charlotte' and *Solidago caesia*, a North American goldenrod that flowers from late summer to mid-autumn.

7. Make a quick border. To provide instant privacy, create a green hedge structure by growing ivy over natural brushwood screening.

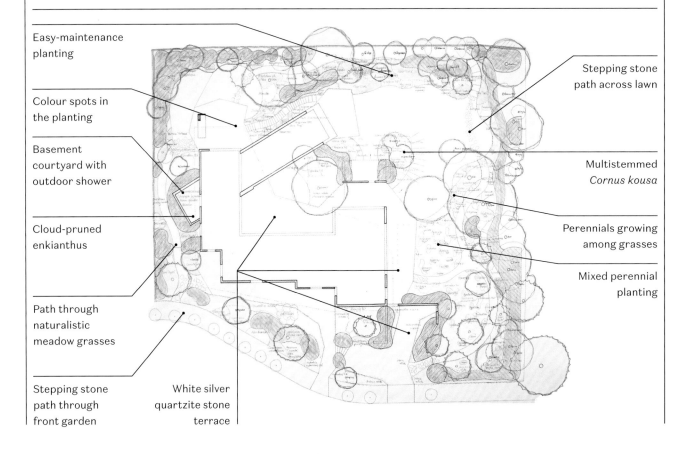

Easy-maintenance planting

Colour spots in the planting

Basement courtyard with outdoor shower

Cloud-pruned enkianthus

Path through naturalistic meadow grasses

Stepping stone path through front garden

White silver quartzite stone terrace

Stepping stone path across lawn

Multistemmed *Cornus kousa*

Perennials growing among grasses

Mixed perennial planting

Polished stone boulders on the white stone terrace with drifts of *Carex lenta* 'Osaka'.

The stepping-stone path through the front garden with *Carex lenta* 'Kyoto' and *Hakonechloa macra* (Japanese forest grass).

A stepping-stone path across the lawn, with *Aster divaricatus* 'Tradescant' and *Carex lenta* 'Osaka' in the border.

The outdoor shower with low-growing ferns, *Isotoma fluviatilis* (blue star creeper) and wild ginger.

The view towards the house through the meadow of *Sesleria autumnalis* (autumn moor-grass), with echinacea in the foreground.

The eating area on the stone terrace in the outdoor kitchen.

NATURAL FORMALITY

The Details

Echinacea purpurea 'Virgin', *Sesleria autumnalis* and *Agastache* 'Blackadder'.

Plantings of *Echinacea purpurea* 'Virgin' by the terrace pick up the dappled light under the trees.

The sloping border with *Persicaria amplexicaulis* 'Firetail' beneath the multistemmed *Cornus kousa*.

CASE STUDY

Statement Steps

SARA JANE ROTHWELL

This wonderful garden, at 1,000sq m (10,800sq ft), wraps around the property, which was built in the 1920s as part of a new garden suburb. The aim of the design was to open up the garden, while also providing privacy from overlooking windows. The redesign takes as its focus a lovely old *Magnolia grandiflora* with its huge leathery leaves and characterful multistemmed trunk. Generous turf steps lead up to the tree and the rusted Corten steel risers are echoed on the left in three feature panels, creating an elegant, minimal feel. At the top of the steps is a hardwood deck that travels around the corner of the house to a broad patio at the rear. Herbaceous borders of blousy mixed plantings soften the edges and give this garden a painterly feel, while yew hedges break up the lines and add a visual link to the dark hedged border.

Closer to the house, the hardwood decks have weathered to a warm grey colour that blends with the pale grey sandstone treads and pearl-grey, non-slip ceramic tiles. Very deep planting beds enable plants to thrive and give of their best, while stepping stones allow for ongoing plant maintenance. There's a balance between planting and pleasure in this garden. The large lawn is softly edged with gently mounding foliage and the trampoline is sunken and hidden behind a mound of ornamental grasses. Seating and dining areas are expansive and inviting. A timber bench, built into a retaining wall, offers permanent seating, while a feature wall comprising hardwood verticals inset with Corten steel brings all the elements together.

Right: Wide turf steps are edged with rusted Corten steel, giving the design a bold yet natural look. The magnificent *Magnolia grandiflora*, with its Japanese-like elegance and gnarled trunk, has become the focal point of the upper garden.

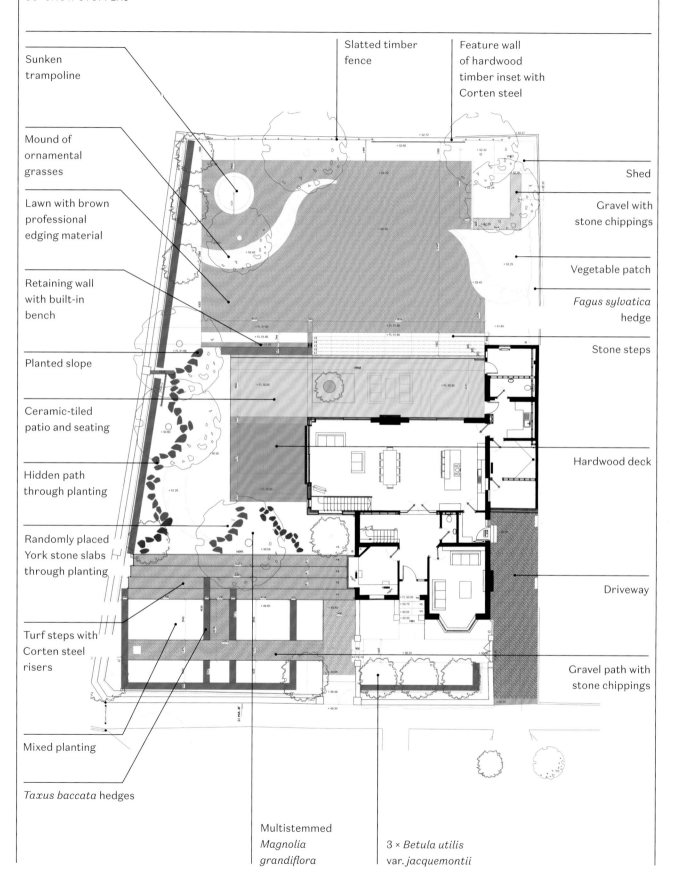

Sunken
trampoline

Slatted timber
fence

Feature wall
of hardwood
timber inset with
Corten steel

Mound of
ornamental
grasses

Shed

Gravel with
stone chippings

Lawn with brown
professional
edging material

Vegetable patch

Fagus sylvatica
hedge

Retaining wall
with built-in
bench

Stone steps

Planted slope

Ceramic-tiled
patio and seating

Hardwood deck

Hidden path
through planting

Randomly placed
York stone slabs
through planting

Driveway

Turf steps with
Corten steel
risers

Gravel path with
stone chippings

Mixed planting

Taxus baccata hedges

Multistemmed
*Magnolia
grandiflora*

3 × *Betula utilis*
var. *jacquemontii*

Design Checklist

1. Waste not, want not. Set aside excavated topsoil to reuse. Here, it has been recycled into sweeping land mounds and to create the wide green turf steps. Rubble-strewn excavations can be used for foundations.

2. Make the most of rusted Corten steel. This highly versatile material has a myriad of different uses and is popular not only because it can be cut into step risers (as here), planters, water tanks or sculptural forms, but also because it works well with other natural colours.

3. Make paths last longer by first laying down a weed-suppressing membrane. Stabilised gravel can be laid on top of this and then topped with small stone chippings in a colour that reflects the surrounding architecture.

4. Hide unattractive elements such as trampolines behind plants. Here, the trampoline has been sunk in the ground and hidden behind a land mound planted with ornamental grasses.

5. Provide access to large mixed planting beds for both gardeners and explorers by creating hidden paths of randomly placed stone slabs that weave through the planting.

6. Make sure the hard structures in your garden earn their keep. In this garden scheme a timber bench (which echoes the hardwood timber deck) has been set into a retaining wall, providing seating for the length of a dining table. Over the years, timber weathers to a lovely soft grey, which will give a warm and natural feel to any garden.

7. Use soft LED strips (available by the roll) to light up a feature, seating area or, as here, a sculptural boundary wall. LEDs transform indoor and outdoor lighting options, giving gardeners much more flexibility.

8. Edge paths and lawns. It might sound old-fashioned, but professionally edged paths and lawns look better and last longer. They also save you having to recut edges by hand. So, overcome prejudice and use a professional edging material to maintain a smart finish.

STATEMENT STEPS

The
Details

Make a feature of a boundary wall. In this scheme, hardwood timber and rusted Corten steel inserts frame a planting of *Deschampsia cespitosa* (tufted hair grass) and pink penstemon.

The flowerheads of *Calamagrostis × acutiflora* 'Karl Foerster' look good all winter. Plant to catch low winter light.

Yew hedging provides a solid green foil for a loose perennial mixed planting of salvia, penstemon and calamagrostis.

Dot the tall and airy *Verbena bonariensis* through plantings to provide height and drama.

A romantic planting of penstemon, *Salvia nemorosa* 'Caradonna' (one of the best forms of salvia) and *Rosa* 'Gertrude Jekyll'.

The turf steps are edged with rusted Corten steel, which immediately turns them into a statement piece.

Contemporary seating with *Penstemon* 'Raven' and the perennial wallflower *Erysimum* 'Bowles's Mauve' planted in the raised bed behind.

Anemanthele lessoniana (pheasant's tail grass) and deep pink persicaria contrast with Corten steel uprights.

2

Family Gardens

CASE STUDY

Formal Diversity

MATT KEIGHTLEY

Sophisticated and subtle, at first glance this looks like a garden for 'grown-ups'. Only by meandering along its length do you discover a space at the back for children, screened by low-level box hedging and three columnar *Cupressus sempervirens* Stricta Group. The simple planting combination not only masks the trampoline, but it provides cover for a dog run. This is ingenious, giving the kids and dog a special area to play in and allowing the adults to retain control of a space unspoilt by unsightly playtime paraphernalia.

Given the relatively narrow space, it is important to utilise the wider landscape by bringing it into the scheme. Existing fences are covered with panels of jasmine to avoid abrupt stops at the garden edge. This simultaneously softens the boundary line, adds interest and leads the eye towards neighbouring trees, so creating a greater feeling of space.

The smart, large-format paving ensures the beds keep their definition, the lawn looks crisp, and balance is retained. The sharp, easy-to-work-to edges are perfect for those anxious about maintenance – a garden is to be enjoyed, not enslave you to a summer of work. Indeed, many clients request a 'low-maintenance' garden, which is possible with a balanced approach. Here this is achieved through the framing of the lawn and the balance of evergreens to perennials (use more of the former for a less labour-intensive garden). The landscaping is on one level, so changes of planting level are crucial for interest, achieved with topiary, boundary screens, rooftop-trained trees, groundcover perennials and *Cupressus* columns.

Right: Panoramic glazing in the rear façade retracts to reveal the perfect lawn and proportions of the space.

FORMAL DIVERSITY

Design Checklist

1. Increase the formality of a space and provide an 'easy-to-work-to' edge for mowing and maintenance by edging the lawn with paving. This also gives definition to the borders and provides a low-maintenance access path around the entire garden.

2. Choose large-format paving to reduce the number of joint lines required in a terrace, giving a clean, contemporary and often minimalist feel to a space. Try different mortar colours before you commit; sometimes I prefer

to go dark and contrast with the stone to show off the impressive format.

3. Create a seamless transition between the interior and exterior by avoiding level changes throughout the hard landscaping. The garden assumes the role of an additional outdoor room.

4. Make the most of narrow beds by employing layered planting. Choose plants that are compact in form, whether ground cover or tall grasses. You can take your levels from 20cm (8in) to 3m (10ft) in a bed only 1.5m (5ft) deep.

5. Create intrigue and encourage a desire to explore via discreet separation. In this garden, this results in individual areas for both parents and children. Play equipment is not often all that aesthetically appealing, so screen it with tactful planting, while retaining views for the safety-conscious.

6. Soften boundaries with a hedge or climbers on a framework to draw in the wider landscape and make your neighbours' trees feel like your own, so creating the illusion of a much larger garden. A softer boundary can also be more aesthetically pleasing than an abrupt, nondescript fence.

7. Improve privacy by planting trees. Trees add height and interest to a scheme. There are infinite space-saving options available, including pleached trees, columns, fans and cordons – so more or less something for any style of garden.

8. Encourage maximum use of a garden with multiple seating arrangements. A secondary seating space gives the user added incentive to pay repeat visits to another area of the garden. Adding a bench will give you a vantage point of the house or garden that was previously unexploited.

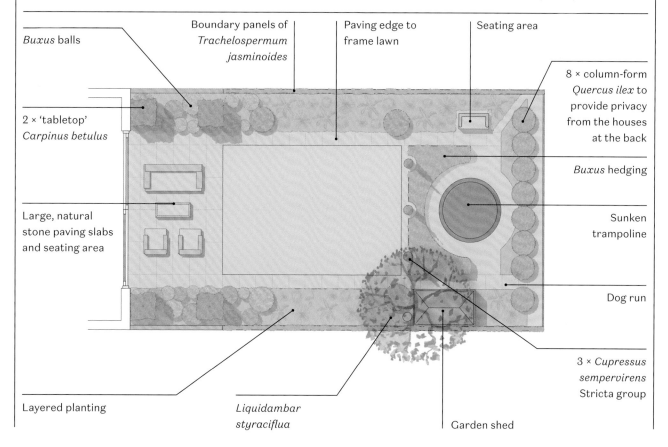

Buxus balls

Boundary panels of Trachelospermum jasminoides

Paving edge to frame lawn

Seating area

8 × column-form Quercus ilex to provide privacy from the houses at the back

2 × 'tabletop' Carpinus betulus

Buxus hedging

Large, natural stone paving slabs and seating area

Sunken trampoline

Dog run

3 × Cupressus sempervirens Stricta group

Layered planting

Liquidambar styraciflua

Garden shed

FORMAL DIVERSITY

The Details

Layered planting in a shady corner provides depth in a relatively narrow border, from groundcover ferns right up to the top tier of the silver-leaved dogwood, *Cornus alternifolia* 'Argentea'.

The panoramic glazed façade frames the vista from the living space into the garden. When retracted, this creates a seamless transition.

A bench among the planting is out of sight from the house, but a welcome discovery at the end of the garden.

A multifunctional strip of paving edges the lawn, defines the planted border and also provides a clear and practical path to the rear of the garden.

Elegant lounge furniture basks in a wash of warm, ambient light from the house.

Calamagrostis × *acutiflora* 'Karl Foerster' in a perennial bed and tall *Carpinus* above structured planting.

Ground lights accentuate the form and provide a warm glow at the base of the *Cupressus sempervirens* Stricta Group.

Classic colours used in a contemporary way, as the heads of *Sanguisorba* 'Tanna' float and bounce above white *Rosa* 'Iceberg'.

Fitting It All In

SEAN WALTER

It is hard to believe that so much can be squeezed into a small, urban back garden without everything feeling cramped. Sean Walter of The Plant Specialist has managed to achieve this with the careful placement of all the elements, using one as a foil for the next to provide contrast and definition. The dining area, close to the house, is uncluttered and formal, and underpinned by the stone-flagged terrace. From here, gravel paths lead to the studio at the end of the garden and also a wooden deck, which is hidden behind the large prairie bed and the massed plantings of *Hakonechloa macra* (Japanese forest grass). All the perennials are planted in this one large flowerbed, which creates real impact but also allows for successional flowering, from spring bulbs through to autumn grasses. Opposite, on the far side of the lawn, the line of clipped yew columns screens out the neighbouring garden. The height of the yews and the gaps between them add to the feeling of space. Restricting the rest of the planting simplifies the design. There is a line of pleached *Carpinus* (hornbeam) along the left-hand fence, which is painted a dark colour so that it disappears into the background. The fence is planted with evergreen *Trachelospermum jasminoides* (star jasmine), while the shady area below is framed with box hedges and lit up with plantings of persicaria. At the back, the studio and deck are encircled with a sea of informal grasses. Evergreen *Pittosporum tobira* complements the mounds of miscanthus and *Hakonechloa macra*, creating an evergreen backdrop.

Left: Site a dining table close to the house to entice you outdoors. *Wisteria sinensis* (Chinese wisteria) is trained over the metal pergola. In the background, evergreen *Trachelospermum jasminoides* (star jasmine) covers the fence and fills the air with its exotic scent at night.

FITTING IT ALL IN

Design Checklist

1. Make the most of the space. Use hard landscaping to define areas and to create and frame views. Contrasting the hard and soft planting (that is, formal hedges with airy perennials) creates drama. Make the most of fences and pergolas by growing climbers over them that soften and extend the greenery, while also providing privacy.

2. Plant large beds. The bed of mixed perennials works so well partly because of its size, which adds impact and allows for successional planting using a variety of species that will provide flower colour from spring through to autumn.

3. Make a prairie garden. An airy planting of mixed perennials is bright and contemporary. This type of planting usually includes grasses as well as flowers. Here, plants include *Echinacea purpurea* 'Magnus Superior', *Stipa gigantea*, *Potentilla nepalensis* 'Miss Willmott', *Perovskia* 'Blue Spire' and *Veronicastrum virginicum* f. *roseum*. Pick tall, narrow plants with little basal growth (like thalictrum, veronicastrum, and sanguisorba), so you can fit more in.

4. Contrast formal and informal. A low box hedge provides a solid green foil to the airy planting and keeps it distinct from the gravel path. In the same way, the shaggy-looking bistort (*Persicaria*), with its broad, sheathed leaves and carmine spikes, balances the stiff uprights of pleached hornbeam.

5. Have it all! Amazingly, this small city garden has space for a shed, lawn, eating terrace, large flowerbed, paths and topiary without looking cluttered. Keep things simple, by defining the requirements for the garden and giving key features generous space.

6. Define the dining area. Siting the table on a terrace adds a sense of space. This is emphasised by the path and lawn that border it, the pots of hosta by the house and the plantings of *Hakonechloa macra* by the large border.

7. Keep edges neat. Crucial to the design where the terrace meets the lawn are the neat edges. The best way to achieve this is to create a mowing strip by edging the lawn with metal, brick or stone.

8. Fade sheds into the background. Most sheds are not architectural gems. Paint them grey or other muted shades.

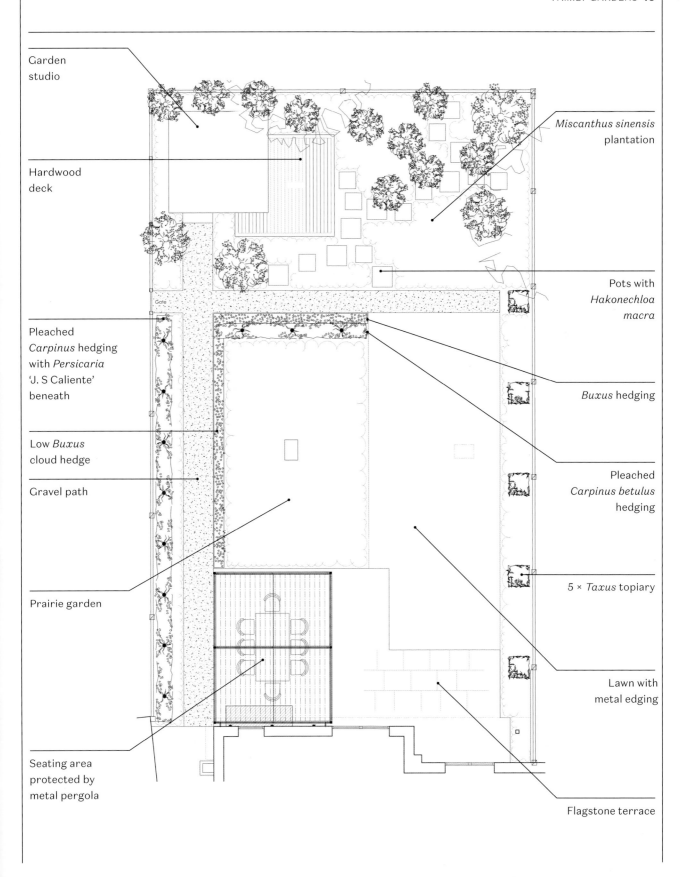

Garden studio

Hardwood deck

Miscanthus sinensis plantation

Pots with *Hakonechloa macra*

Pleached *Carpinus* hedging with *Persicaria* 'J. S Caliente' beneath

Buxus hedging

Low *Buxus* cloud hedge

Gravel path

Pleached *Carpinus betulus* hedging

5 × *Taxus* topiary

Prairie garden

Gate

Seating area protected by metal pergola

Lawn with metal edging

Flagstone terrace

A view looking out onto the
seating area beneath the arbour.

The shed is painted a rich grey tone so
it blends into the background behind
the planting of *Miscanthus sinensis*.

Verbena macdougalii 'Lavender Spires' and *Echinacea purpurea* 'Magnus Superior' in the bed of mixed perennials.

FITTING IT ALL IN

The Details

The deep carmine spires of the bistort, *Persicaria amplexicaulis* 'J S Caliente'.

The flat heads of *Hydrandgea aspera*, with its glaucous, leathery leaves, tone beautifully with the green-painted shed.

Pots planted with the strappy-leaved *Hakonechloa macra* (Japanese forest grass) contrast with the upright yew buttresses to the right of the lawn.

CASE STUDY

Natural Exuberance

CHARLOTTE ROWE

So often a newly built property comes with a compromised garden. In this case, a patio created by the developers was much too large and a wedge-shaped lawn, meanly edged with narrow beds, tapered to a point where an uninspiring summerhouse accentuated the odd shape of the garden. So what is the best solution to a scenario like this?

The owners wanted plenty from their garden of 650sq m (7,000sq ft), including an eating zone and outdoor cooking area, some water, an arbour and a trampoline, not forgetting a fully soundproof room for a keen drummer. The solution is ingenious. The wide rectangular lawn immediately creates width and space, and leads the eye past the drum room (the discreet dark grey timber building with tall narrow windows and a green roof on the left) to an airy arbour complete with a small water feature and fireplace. There is a dining area and built-in barbecue to the right.

The trampoline is almost completely hidden behind large planting beds. These repeat and echo throughout the garden, both front and back, with mounds of sun-loving Mediterranean plants that soften the stone setts and gravel. The garden is screened all around with mature layered hedging, so there is a feeling of complete privacy. The contemporary form of the arbour is beautifully matched by the slim uprights of the flat-topped London plane trees, while next to the house the patio has been replaced by a limestone terrace softened and given definition by the comfortable turquoise seating and an area of gravel planting.

Right: Planting beds link the terrace with the lawn, softening the rectangular geometry with effusive plantings of mixed perennials. A palette of lime greens, blues and purples runs through the beds, bringing unity to the design.

NATURAL EXUBERANCE

Design Checklist

1. Plant pleached trees. The *Platanus × hispanica* (London Plane tree) avenue in this garden shows how useful trained specimens can be, especially in a small space. They are practical as well as sculptural and look great uplit at night.

2. Cloud prune evergreen balls of *Prunus lusitanica* (Portugal laurel), *Buxus* (box), *Taxus* (yew) and *Ilex crenata* (box-leaved holly) add a formal character to the planting. The technique can be used on existing evergreens and hedges, as well as individual plants.

3. Consider pruning trees to keep them within the bounds of a small garden as with these flat topped plane trees leading to an urn on a pedestal.

4. Make lighting work. Subtle uplighting makes the avenue come alive at night, while also giving height to the space.

5. Trick the eye. Breaking up odd-shaped spaces into smaller 'zones' regularises an oddly shaped plot. Here, it makes the garden appear and feel much larger than it was before.

6. Create privacy by planting a boundary screen of layered hedging, with contrasting light and dark foliage of mature beech and yew.

7. Choose a palette. By using the same palette of colours – here lime greens and purples – the planting helps to unify the space.

8. Contrast formal and informal. Here, a raised stone wall contrasts with billowing planting to maintain a sense of formality along the gravel path.

9. Use accessories to add colour. Use furniture to create a link between inside and outside. Here, the bold contemporary shapes of the turquoise seating draw the eye from inside the house and across the lawn, acting as a link between indoors and outside.

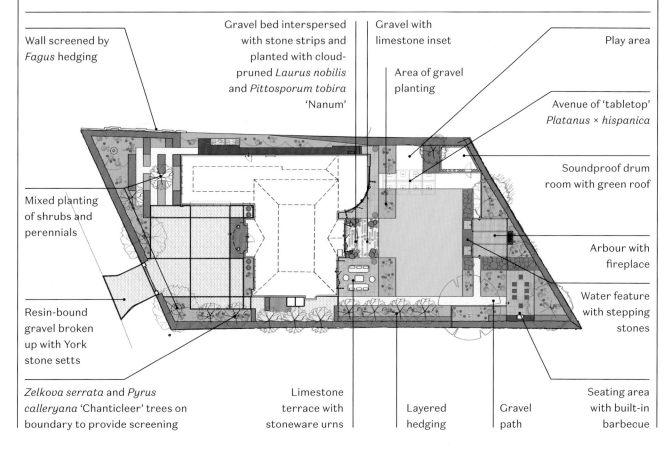

Wall screened by *Fagus* hedging

Gravel bed interspersed with stone strips and planted with cloud-pruned *Laurus nobilis* and *Pittosporum tobira* 'Nanum'

Gravel with limestone inset

Area of gravel planting

Play area

Avenue of 'tabletop' *Platanus × hispanica*

Soundproof drum room with green roof

Mixed planting of shrubs and perennials

Arbour with fireplace

Water feature with stepping stones

Resin-bound gravel broken up with York stone setts

Zelkova serrata and *Pyrus calleryana* 'Chanticleer' trees on boundary to provide screening

Limestone terrace with stoneware urns

Layered hedging

Gravel path

Seating area with built-in barbecue

NATURAL EXUBERANCE

The Details

Tucking the barbecue into the 'point' of the garden uses and hides an awkward area of the space.

An avenue of tabletop-shaped plane trees edges a gravel path while also screening the drum room.

The wood stack in the side of the fireplace adds colour, texture and visual 'warmth'.

The water feature with stepping stones provides fun and dramatic interest.

The gravel beds are interspersed with stone strips and mounds of sun-loving Mediterranean plants.

A large stoneware urn adds architectural form to the loose planting of salvia, euphorbia and lavender.

Subtle lighting accentuates the forms of the pear trees and magnolia, while layered hedging softens the boundary.

The distinctive, globe-shaped heads of alliums, which are planted with leathery rodgersia, provide architectural form even after the flowers have faded.

The bespoke soundproof drum room was built to fit into the oddly wedge-shaped part of the garden.

Contemporary Relaxed

JANE BROCKBANK

This garden needed to satisfy a range of requirements. First, it had to complement the newly built traditional-style town house. Second, it had to create the feeling of a contemporary but informal English country garden and, while balancing both those requirements, it also had to provide somewhere for children to play. The original garden had a swimming pool, fountains and, unfortunately, a heavy × *Cuprocyparis leylandii* (Leyland cypress), as well as four out-of-fashion mature poplars. The space looked exhausted and uninspiring. At 35 × 25m (115 × 82ft) it was, however, a good size. The local council allowed the designer, Jane Brockbank, to take out the cypress, but the poplars had to stay. The swimming pool and fountains went, too.

The design of the new garden blends luxuriant plantings in generous beds with a large lawn, both of which can be seen from the terrace. The fire bowl provides both sculptural interest and warmth on cool evenings, while the four *Sorbus commixta* (Japanese rowan) define the space and restrict the visual impact of the new-build house behind. The whole design is set on a central axis: the gravel path that leads from the terrace to the lawn. Loose plantings of perennials tumble over its edge. In spring, the key colours are blues. In midsummer, the palette moves to pinks. Three fastigiate box columns in each of the two asymmetrical beds provide winter structure. Hidden paths curve through the flower beds, which are fun for children to run through and ideal for maintenance. Lastly, there is a playhouse and climbing frame.

Left: The Japanese rowans, with their filigree canopy, soften the brickwork of the house. In the centre of the terrace sits a sculptural fire bowl. From the terrace, the adults can watch the children on the lawn beyond the flowerbeds.

CONTEMPORARY RELAXED

Design Checklist

1. Get trees in the ground as soon as possible. Here, *Liquidambar styraciflua* (sweet gum), *Acer rubrum* (red maple), *Prunus avium* (wild cherry) and *Crataegus × lavalleei* 'Carrierei' were planted at the back of the garden while the house was being built. This gave them time to settle in and helped give the new garden a sense of maturity.

2. Save money on expensive playhouses. Children grow out of them quickly, so a cheaper tent-style structure could be a better option.

3. Abandon unwanted features. Swimming pools and fountains can be more trouble than they're worth. Removing them can be a big job but worth it if the feature doesn't suit your design.

4. Be pragmatic. Builders often compact soil or park heavy machinery right in the middle of a bed, while architects rarely allow for beds deep enough to take the amount of soil that plants need to survive. Be prepared to adapt. The four *Sorbus commixta* (Japanese rowan) trees planted here had to have their roots restricted, but the upside is that this restrains their growth, which is beneficial here.

5. Choose the right paving. The Catcastle Grey paving on the terrace comes from a single quarry in Yorkshire. It is not cheap, but each stone has unique markings and tones, so it creates a very special surface and is really worth using in small areas of a garden, such as on a terrace, to make an impact.

6. Choose tough plants near children's play areas to withstand whatever comes their way. Delicate, wispy grasses and perennials may be destroyed by enthusiastic games. The wide gravel path visually separates plants from footballs.

7. Be safe with fires and children. The switch that turns on the gas in the fire bowl should be carefully sited – high up and well out of the way of children.

8. Use similar coloured flowers in the bed for impact. In early summer, the flowers in the central flowerbeds are all blue (*Iris* 'Jane Phillips', *Salvia nemorosa* 'Caradonna' and *Geranium* Rozanne). From midsummer onwards the focus is pink, with eryngiums, sedums, *Astrantia major* 'Claret' and *Saponaria × lempergii* 'Max Frei'.

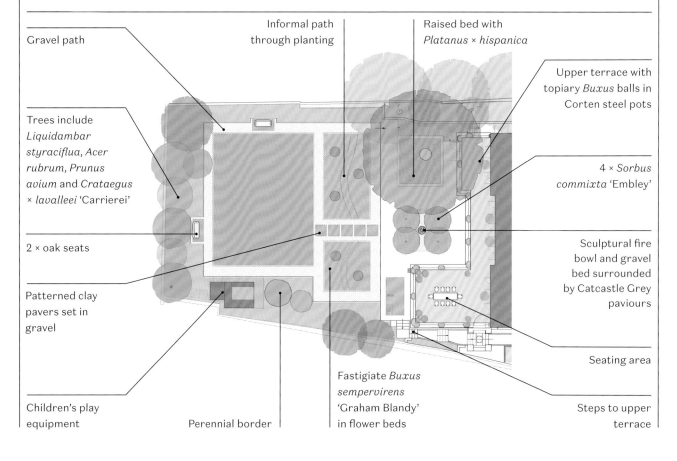

Gravel path

Informal path through planting

Raised bed with *Platanus × hispanica*

Trees include *Liquidambar styraciflua*, *Acer rubrum*, *Prunus avium* and *Crataegus × lavalleei* 'Carrierei'

Upper terrace with topiary *Buxus* balls in Corten steel pots

4 × *Sorbus commixta* 'Embley'

2 × oak seats

Sculptural fire bowl and gravel bed surrounded by Catcastle Grey paviours

Patterned clay pavers set in gravel

Children's play equipment

Perennial border

Fastigiate *Buxus sempervirens* 'Graham Blandy' in flower beds

Seating area

Steps to upper terrace

Perennial beds planted with white *Allium nigrum*, acid-green *Euphorbia palustris* and purple *Salvia nemorosa* 'Caradonna'.

The dark grey hue of the contemporary outdoor rattan furniture perfectly complements the tan brick of the house.

The Japanese rowan, *Sorbus commixta* 'Embley', on the terrace that overlooks the perennial beds.

The perennial marguerite, *Anthemis* 'Susanna Mitchell', is used as a foil for the summer planting.

Fastigiate box in the flower beds adds structure and helps maintain the design through winter.

CONTEMPORARY RELAXED

The Details

Magenta *Paeonia* (peonies), *Melica altissima* 'Alba' and *Papaver orientale* (oriental poppy) add pops of colour.

A wooden seat from Gaze Burvill with delicate, white *Libertia grandiflora* in the foreground.

Patterned clay pavers are set like stepping stones on the main path from the terrace to the lawn.

The elegant topiary box shapes in Corten steel pots are a play on the traditional country garden.

CASE STUDY

A Wildlife Garden

JANE BROCKBANK

It is difficult to believe that this garden, with its natural swimming pond and wildlife meadow, is only a few miles from the centre of London, and that it was only created relatively recently. The brief to the designer, Jane Brockbank, was to create an informal garden that all the family could enjoy and that is also good for wildlife. Although the garden was originally quite overgrown and required work, it had a superb position backing onto a park containing lots of trees, providing a natural screen. The plot's other distinct advantage was that an extension was added to the house at the same time as the garden was created, which meant that the floor could be laid so the interior flowed seamlessly outdoors.

The eating area is separated from the poolside terrace by a timber raised bed that brims with a mono planting of grasses that look sculptural all year round. The same timber is used for the boardwalk that leads across the shallow margins at one end of the swimming pond. A large Kadai firepit is popular with the older teenagers, while there's also an athletic field, trampoline, swings, table-tennis table and three-room treehouse to keep the other children entertained. The treehouse is made from a mixture of new and reclaimed wood, and fixed to a mature willow, so the large weeping branches soften its edges. The wildflower meadow works both to frame the play areas and to mirror the natural plantings at the edges of the swimming pond.

Right: The sunny garden has heavy clay soil. The mixed planting thus includes clay-tolerant perennials such as *Geranium* Rozanne, *Libertia grandiflora, Cirsium rivulare* and *Aconitum* 'Ivorine'. The pond can be heated to extend the swimming season.

A WILDLIFE GARDEN

Design Checklist

1. Add a wildflower area to a small garden. A mixture of slow-growing grasses and wild flowers was used in this garden. The area was underplanted with spring bulbs, then left to grow long until midsummer when it is mown regularly. This is a good option for small to medium-sized gardens, where a full-scale meadow would look too ragged in summer, or where the soil is too rich for a more flowery meadow.

2. Convert a lawn into a meadow by first stopping feeding and applying weedkiller. Mow weekly in the first year to weaken the grass. Gradually, local wild plants will establish.

3. Improve your soil to give your plants the best start in life. Different soils will require different treatments but most will benefit from a mulch of well-rotted organic matter.

4. Select fixed or flexible treehouse fixings. Flexible joints are attached to the support beam, but allow the tree to move in the wind. Do not use screws or nails to secure beams. Most professionals now use Tree Attachment Bolts (TABs). Get someone with professional expertise to erect your treehouse and ask an approved arboriculturist to check the suitability of the tree before going ahead.

5. Install a swimming pond to attract birds, insects and amphibians into your garden. Swimming ponds come in a range of types, from natural wild swimming ponds, with curved, pond-like edges, to the rectangular design shown here. Unlike traditional swimming pools, they look interesting all year round. Swimming ponds need to be installed by a specialist contractor.

6. Encourage wildlife by leaving shallow areas at the edge of the water, so that animals can climb in and out easily. Partially submerged rocks and pebbles are ideal. Provide plants with upright stems for emerging damselfly and dragonfly nymphs.

7. Choose a firepit for keeping warm on chilly evenings or for cooking. Firepits come in almost every form imaginable; there is a size, style and price point for every garden. Obviously, if there are children around, ensure the firepit has a sturdy frame so that it cannot topple over. You should also provide a cover.

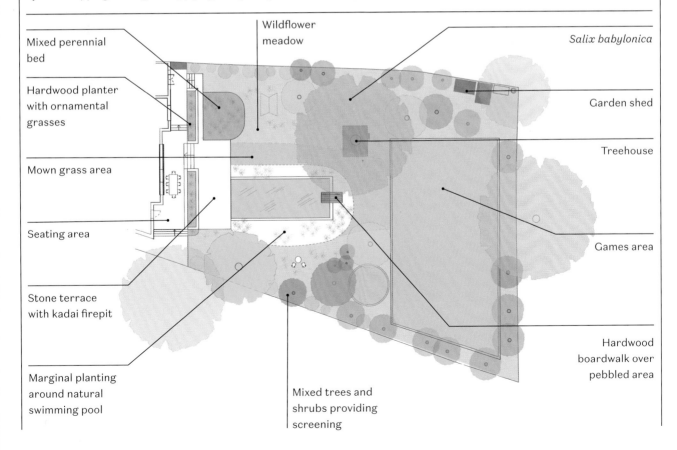

Mixed perennial bed

Hardwood planter with ornamental grasses

Mown grass area

Seating area

Stone terrace with kadai firepit

Marginal planting around natural swimming pool

Wildflower meadow

Mixed trees and shrubs providing screening

Salix babylonica

Garden shed

Treehouse

Games area

Hardwood boardwalk over pebbled area

A WILDLIFE GARDEN

The
Details

Mixed perennials, including *Alchemilla mollis* (lady's mantle), *Verbena bonariensis* and *Libertia grandiflora*.

At night lighting shines through the reeds that grow at the margins of the natural swimming pond.

Meadow grasses and wild flowers surround the games area.

The swimming pond is sheltered and given privacy by mature trees.

The natural timber boardwalk crosses the pebbled shallow area of the natural swimming pond.

Spires of white *Aconitum* 'Ivorine' with tall, purple *Verbena bonariensis*.

Myosotis palustris (water forget-me-not) at the end of the pond.

CASE STUDY

Simple Chic

SARA JANE ROTHWELL

At face value this seems a wonderfully serene and simple design, but its structure is carefully underpinned by balancing forms, styles and textures. There is a calm reassurance in the repeating rectangles of the lawn, the zinc panel with its blue-grey patina, and the almost-black pools. Pale stone planks of sawn grey sandstone form dynamic edges, and paths stride purposefully, yet everything is softened and merges with the planting. This is achieved by using a coherent palette of colours across the garden – greens and whites, soft greys, purples, blues and mauves and, here and there, a strong accent of magenta. In spring, bulbs emerge, giving a blast of brights to kick off the season. As with all Sara Jane Rothwell's gardens, what is beautiful is wherever possible also practical, so the beds contain hidden stone steps to allow gardeners to look after the plants. Even the weathered zinc panel has space behind it where cushions from the built-in timber bench can be stored. The garden also echoes the property, a brick London townhouse with strong contemporary features, notably the floor-to-ceiling steel windows that look out from the kitchen to the garden. At night the owners can look over the lawn from the house towards the underlit water feature. A row of young amelanchier trees on the left is gently uplit, drawing the eye along the side wall. Their silhouettes are just as strong in winter as summer, with a firepit enabling the owners to continue enjoying the shortening evenings.

Right: The underlying geometry of the design brings this garden together. The shapes and forms of the soft and hard landscaping repeat and echo in the rectangles of the green lawn and the zinc rear panel, as well as in the lines made by the paths and water feature.

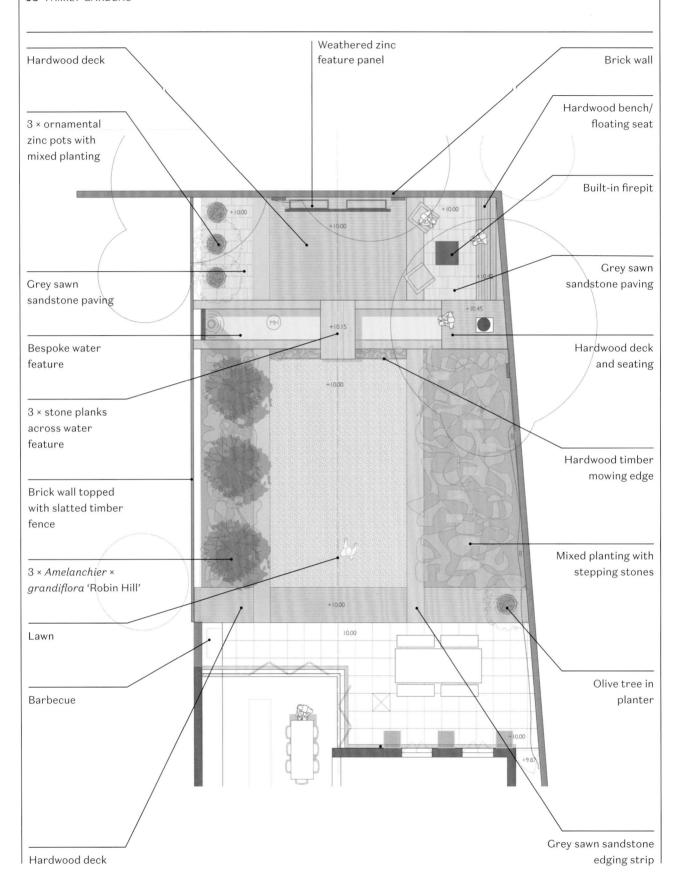

Hardwood deck

3 × ornamental zinc pots with mixed planting

Grey sawn sandstone paving

Bespoke water feature

3 × stone planks across water feature

Brick wall topped with slatted timber fence

3 × *Amelanchier × grandiflora* 'Robin Hill'

Lawn

Barbecue

Hardwood deck

Weathered zinc feature panel

Brick wall

Hardwood bench/ floating seat

Built-in firepit

Grey sawn sandstone paving

Hardwood deck and seating

Hardwood timber mowing edge

Mixed planting with stepping stones

Olive tree in planter

Grey sawn sandstone edging strip

SIMPLE CHIC

Design Checklist

1. Create drama with carefully positioned lighting, as here with these three fastigiate *Amelanchier × grandiflora* 'Robin Hill'. By uplighting the water wall and the deck at the end of the garden, a sense of depth and space is created, linking the garden to the house.

2. Achieve the lived-in look. The zinc panel on the rear wall has been coated with a protective T-Wash to create an instant effect of aged metal. The lovely, soft grey-blue of the panel is then picked up in the palette of blues and mauves in the planting.

3. Work out where the sun falls at different times of the day. Here, the deck hugs the boundary wall and so seating has been placed where it will catch the evening sun.

4. Give the garden a natural effervescence by providing a structure of evergreen shrubs interplanted with herbaceous perennials and highlights of seasonal colour.

5. Keep what you can. Take time to figure out what works and what you really cannot abide. An existing fence can be spruced up with a lick of new paint or transformed with new climbers. If possible, untie any climbers that you want to retain or prune them back in order to allow for repainting the fence.

6. Cover brick walls with climbers to soften and 'green' the boundaries. Here, jasmine and campsis have been trained along one of the walls, while an existing rose was retained and rambles through a green wall of ivy. When choosing roses always check that they won't be too large for the space.

7. Find the best varieties of the plants you like. Look out for plants that have been awarded an AGM (Award of Garden Merit). This is the Royal Horticultural Society equivalent to a Michelin star and is given to plants that have been shown to do well in most gardens and that are strong, reliable and have good disease resistance.

8. Go for the 'wow!' factor. Choose flowers that excite you. Designing a garden is a little like styling an interior, so think about contrasts and textures. Here, plummy *Penstemon* 'Raven' is paired with fine, purple-stemmed *Salvia nemorosa* 'Caradonna' and the acid-green, floral puffs of *Alchemilla mollis* (lady's mantle). These are all great garden-worthy plants.

SIMPLE CHIC

The Details

The contemporary water-wall fountain creates constant sound and motion as it falls.

Verbena bonariensis copes well in many conditions and is here combined with *Selinum wallichianum*.

Bright cushions encourage you to sit on the built-in timber bench.

A stone mowing strip separates the lawn from the bed, which is spilling over with *Alchemilla mollis* (lady's mantle).

The pools are divided by an elegant bridge of three stone planks.

Water lilies come in many colours and sizes. Choose a small-leaved variety for a small pool.

The zinc-coated, galvanized-steel water wall, which is 1.8m (6ft) tall, pours water into the pool when activated.

This storage panel has ample space behind it for storing the bench cushions in winter.

CASE STUDY

A Natural Swimming Pond

JO THOMPSON

This garden brilliantly creates the impression of a quiet rural idyll. Reeds and trees are reflected in the dark water, while the timber decking and quiet oak pavilion add to the sense that you are in a small country garden in the South of England. The garden was created by award-winning designer Jo Thompson and was originally shown at the RHS Chelsea Flower Show in 2015. It is centred around a large natural swimming pond that Jo planted with *Iris laevigata* (Japanese water iris), floating waterlilies and other water-loving plants. Above, *Betula nigra* (river birch) move in the breeze, while acers are a great choice of smaller tree with their delicate tracery of leaves. The surrounding garden is packed with roses and peonies in varying shades of pink, while tall spires of pale *Digitalis* (foxglove) bring light to the shade in spring. The spiral sculpture is made from Purbeck limestone and acts as a foil to the tumbling verdancy, while also picking up on the pale timber decking. Its shape makes you think of an ammonite, entirely appropriate as this area on the Dorset coast is famous for fossils. The pavilion was inspired by the idea of a writer's retreat, a place to hide from the noise of the world. Jo was particularly inspired by the writing retreats of, among others, Vita Sackville-West and Virginia Woolf. The upper floor is reached via a wooden ladder. Simple natural materials work with the cottage-style planting to make a garden that calms the senses. And, best of all, you can swim in the self-cleaning pond, which is filtered by a broad margin of aquatic plants.

Left: Jo Thompson's garden was shown at the RHS Chelsea Flower Show in 2015. The idea was to create a retreat to escape from daily life. It succeeds brilliantly, creating a space that looks natural, but also works as a family garden.

A NATURAL SWIMMING POND

Design Checklist

1. Use local materials when building garden structures. The garden here, originally created for the 2015 RHS Chelsea Flower Show, was designed to blend into the landscape of the Kent and Sussex Weald where the designer, Jo Thompson, lives. The pavilion was constructed of oak and leads off across the water on pale timber decking.

2. Transform an unwanted swimming pool into a natural swimming pond. It may need relining and the width reduced slightly to allow for marginal planting. Even stagnant ponds can be brought to life as swimming ponds.

3. Select a natural swimming pond to suit your garden. For a more formal garden there are rectangular pools without plants. Or you can plant up the margins of an organically shaped pond with reeds, iris and natural water plants, such as *Mentha aquatica* (water mint), to attract birds and dragonflies.

4. Seek professional advice to ensure your swimming pond is easy to maintain and that the water is kept clear. Pool technology is constantly developing, and these days you can have a completely chemical-free pool that is cleaned using fine-mesh filters and ultraviolet light.

5. Choose plants that reflect the property and location. A natural swimming pond does not have to look like a wildlife pond. A smart contemporary choice might be to create a hedge around a rectangular pool with a mono planting of grasses or lavender.

6. Soften edges with herbaceous plantings. In this garden, spires of *Digitalis* (foxgloves) and verbascum feature in a mixed planting of pale blue *Amsonia tabernaemontana* var. *salicifolia* (eastern bluestar), while the roses, Chianti and 'Louise Odier', give a lovely scent as you walk past.

7. Don't forget trees and shrubs, which can provide a middle and upper storey. They will also help give you privacy from neighbours. However, trees and shrubs are best set back from the edge of the water so that too many leaves don't fall into the pond.

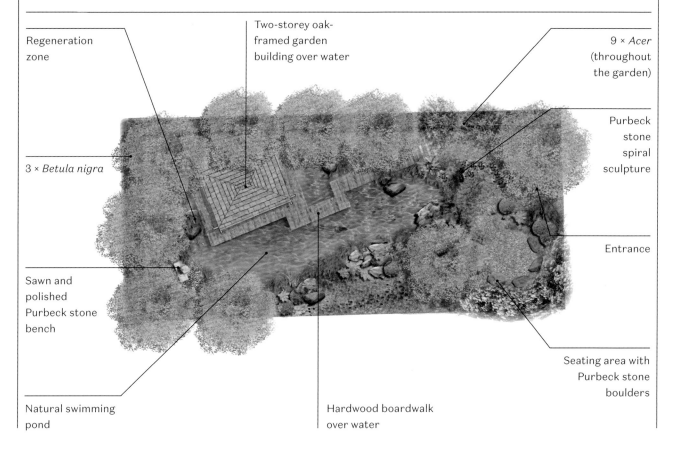

Regeneration zone

3 × *Betula nigra*

Sawn and polished Purbeck stone bench

Natural swimming pond

Two-storey oak-framed garden building over water

Hardwood boardwalk over water

9 × *Acer* (throughout the garden)

Purbeck stone spiral sculpture

Entrance

Seating area with Purbeck stone boulders

Purbeck limestone was used for the ammonite-like spiral sculpture by the edge of the pond.

Timber decking is kind underfoot and also blends into the surroundings.

Lychnis flos-cuculi (ragged robin) and *Iris pallida* thrive on the banks of the natural pond.

Nymphaea (waterlilies) planted alongside the timber decking.

The Details

Lysimachia atropurpurea 'Beaujolais' echoes the upright forms of *Digitalis purpurea* (common foxglove).

A simple stone-block seat is positioned beneath a purple *Acer palmatum* with *Rosa* 'Tuscany Superb'.

The oak pavilion provides shelter, somewhere to relax and changing facilities beside the swimming pond.

3

Minimalist Gardens

Effortless Serenity

MATT KEIGHTLEY

Elegant and fluid, this garden is serene and sophisticated. The restrained approach to the design, in terms of both the planting palette and the material choices, makes for an immaculately understated finish that is pleasing to the eye from all angles. This is a garden that feels just as exciting to look at as it is to walk through. The boardwalk runs the entire length of the space and provides a physical pause before you enter the main garden.

Although muted in tone, the hard-landscaping materials are stunning. Marbling and natural veining in the grey York stone bring depth and intensity to the structure of the garden. Subtle changes in the materials cleverly indicate transitions from one area to the next and, importantly, offer superb textural qualities as you move through the space.

Attempting a restrained planting palette is always brave, but when executed with the right balance of texture, form and colour, it can be magical. This palette is designed to provide punches of bold colour that lead the eye across the garden in spring, with the *Taxus* (yew) hedge and beautiful magnolia specimens standing tall and framing certain views. The paired-variety (of pine and yew), cloud-form hedging works very well with the choice of hard-landscaping materials – a classic case of 'less is more'.

Just to look at the garden is calming; it is somewhere you can use for quiet contemplation and a space that encourages you to enter and meander. This feeling is further enhanced by the tranquil sound of moving water as it slides over the surface of a carved granite wall and enters the expansive rill. The flowing water is mesmerising to watch.

Left: To fully appreciate this garden requires patience. It has bold evergreen and architectural forms and provides bursts of seasonal interest all year.

EFFORTLESS SERENITY

Design Checklist

1. Adjust levels through the structure of the planting. The hard surfaces here are level so that users have an effortless journey through the garden, so depth and layers have been provided through the planting.

2. Opt for restrained planting. This can be incredibly effective if the choices are considered carefully. Think about creating year-round interest with evergreen structure, perennial colour, and layers and levels through the trees and shrubs.

3. Use trees to add height and frame views. A combination of multistemmed and standard forms works well to provide variety, while lifted crowns prevent views being obstructed. Deciduous trees are a sensible choice to avoid blocking out the light during the colder months.

4. Cloud-prune evergreen shrubs. Cloud-pruned shrubs undulate throughout the garden and provide fluidity and movement in ways that grasses and perennials cannot offer. They provide strong structure without adding a sense of traditional formality.

5. Use water to create excitement, intrigue and a focal point in any size of garden. It should be utilised for its atmospheric and reflective qualities, in the ways it both creates relaxing sounds and bounces light and shadow around a space. It is integral to this garden.

6. Choose large-format paving for an impressive and more expansive-looking terrace area. The joints have not been grouted, which not only allows surface water to percolate through but also produces a shadow gap, so emphasizing the scale and beauty of the natural stone and providing visual interest.

7. Think about how and where you enter a garden. This can make a huge difference to the ways in which a space is visualised and used. Here, the boardwalk frames the width of the garden, providing the option of either entering the space at once or pacing up and down the width and appreciating it from a distance.

8. Create atmosphere and drama through the immaculate finishing of the garden space. It feels like a privilege every time you move through this garden and it encourages users to appreciate every detail.

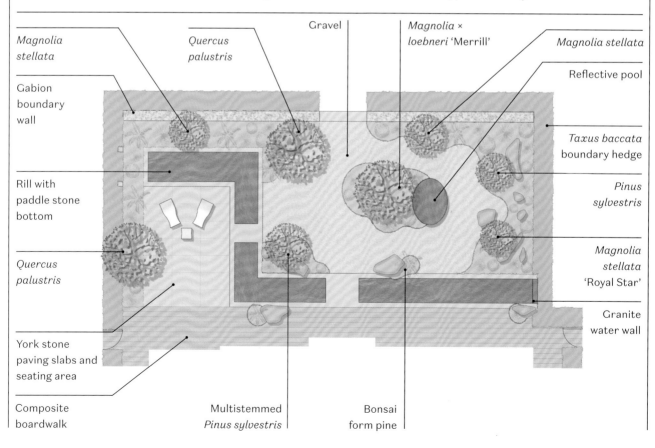

Magnolia stellata

Quercus palustris

Gravel

Magnolia × loebneri 'Merrill'

Magnolia stellata

Gabion boundary wall

Reflective pool

Taxus baccata boundary hedge

Rill with paddle stone bottom

Pinus sylvestris

Quercus palustris

Magnolia stellata 'Royal Star'

York stone paving slabs and seating area

Granite water wall

Composite boardwalk

Multistemmed Pinus sylvestris

Bonsai form pine

Iris 'Pansy Purple', a Siberian flag iris, is a beacon of colour against the muted backdrop of the hard landscaping.

Drifts of iris meander through the garden and burst out of hidden gaps in the structural planting of pines and *Taxus* (yew).

Pinus mugo (dwarf mountain pine) bridges the interface between the stone and the boardwalk.

A structural boulder sits at the foot of a bonsai-form pine, as if to create a pocket-sized natural landscape.

The Details

A water wall is the source for a linear rill that flows through the entire garden, encouraging users to explore the space both visually and physically.

A hypnotic and tranquil pool of jet-black water reflects the mature trees in the wider landscape. This is a part of the garden that compels you to contemplate quietly.

Water flows mesmerisingly down the surface of the carved granite face of the water wall.

Subtle texture is achieved in the rill using river-washed paddlestones and the reflections of a magnolia.

CASE STUDY

City Courtyard Garden

ANDREW WILSON & GAVIN MCWILLIAM

Frequent winners of RHS awards for their show gardens, Andrew Wilson and Gavin McWilliam have taken the quiet elegance of the interior of this town house as the inspiration for its outdoor spaces. There are two areas: a small front garden and a slightly, though not much, larger courtyard at the back. The walls of the house are painted white, which helps to lighten this shaded area. Stone, metal and wood have been used for their textured and weathered surfaces in a palette of warm greys and a powerful charred black. The owners wanted to use the garden for entertaining, so it was important to maximise the amount of available space. A key view is through the large Crittall doors. These look out from the kitchen towards the clean line of pleached *Carpinus* (hornbeam) planted against the silken black walls, which are clad in charred larch using an ancient Japanese technique that is now available in other countries. The randomly distorted vertical panels, some inset with brass, draw in the viewer. Joseph Giles handles provide a subtle design feature on the walls while the polished bronze rings that make up the bespoke tree grilles gleam like jewels. Every surface has been considered, from the smooth grey trunks of the pleached hornbeam to the smooth, black basalt tiles. At night small spotlights set in the floor tiles light up the charred larch screen, while downlighters hidden in the trees illuminate the tree grilles.

Left: In spring and summer, the soft green leaves of the pleached *Carpinus* (hornbeam) unfurl. In autumn, the leaves turn a rich copper that lasts through most of winter. This winter colouring picks up the bright bronze rings of the tree grilles and the brass bands in the charred larch cladding.

CITY COURTYARD GARDEN

Design Checklist

1. Restrict the design to a small palette of materials, textures and tones, and choose the best quality that you can afford. Less is more. Floor tiles, walls and screens all take on a significant role in a minimalist landscape. Each needs to work with and offset the others in terms of both texture and colour.

2. Design the space around a piece of art. The distinctive tree grilles in this garden were made by the London-based sculptor Tom Price. The melted bronze rings provide the interest that might otherwise be lacking in a garden without flowers.

3. Make every surface count in a small garden. In this garden, the wall of the house has been painted grey, which helps it recede into the background. The floor tiles are a flame-finished black basalt. Choose large tiles for a small area to give the illusion of space.

4. Provide a contemporary structural backdrop. Nowadays pleached hornbeam can be bought ready to use. *Carpinus* (hornbeam) has attractive bright green leaves that turn a rich copper in autumn. They can be bought containerised all year round or with rootballs in autumn.

5. Opt for charred timber cladding. This has its origins in an ancient Japanese technique that provides a beautiful and long-lasting product. Finishes can vary enormously, from sleek and contemporary to an almost fragile, highly charred look. Many timbers can be used for this technique, including oak, cedar and ebony. Here, larch has been charred to a black finish.

6. Ensure light fittings are discreet. In this garden, floor lights have been set into the basalt stone tiles to illuminate the charred larch screen, picking out the brass strips. Downlighters hidden in the trees illuminate the bespoke tree grilles. The aim of the design is that you experience the ambience of the lighting without noticing the fittings.

7. Choose weather-resistent garden furniture. UV-stabilised synthetic rattan can be left outside all year round. The light aluminium frame of the rattan-effect modular sofa and chairs in this garden is easy to move and does not rust, while the removable fabric covers allow for easy upkeep.

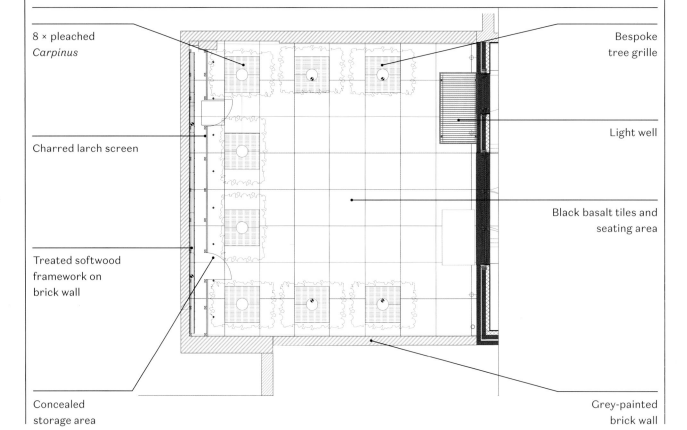

8 × pleached *Carpinus*

Charred larch screen

Treated softwood framework on brick wall

Concealed storage area

Bespoke tree grille

Light well

Black basalt tiles and seating area

Grey-painted brick wall

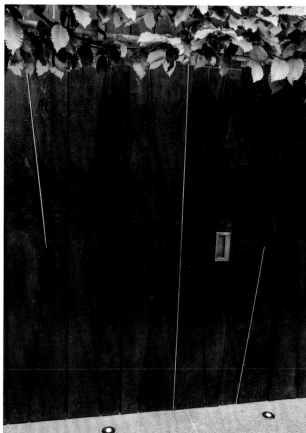

Contemporary seating completes the design. Opt for modular pieces that can be rearranged to suit the occasion.

The charred larch screen with its smart brass inserts below a row of pleached *Carpinus* (hornbeam) trees.

A Corten steel panel mounted on the wall in the front garden.

The tree grilles were made by London-based sculptor Tom Price and set into the black basalt terrace.

Molinia caerulea subsp. *caerulea* 'Heidebraut', a variety of moor-grass, creates swaying movement in the rusted Corten steel planter.

CITY COURTYARD GARDEN

The Details

In the front garden, the slatted back fence and storage box are designed to blend in with the rusted Corten steel planter and warm-coloured paving.

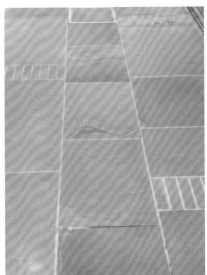

The paving in the front garden is Woodkirk York stone.

CASE STUDY

Verdant Courtyard

MATT KEIGHTLEY

Clean, contemporary lines run through this open-plan interior and continue seamlessly into the garden. The kitchen and garden work as one, with the garden treated as an extension to the living space and framed in its entirety by the impressive floor-to-ceiling glass façade. This is an exciting space full of interest: bold geometry, form and the innovative use of materials. The transition between the spaces is effortless, largely because attention has been paid to every last detail – the wall colours match inside and out, the cupboard shapes are replicated in the 'floating' wall-mounted stones, and even the green Chesterfield sofa is accented by the same deep green of the *Taxus* (yew) hedging units.

The soft- and hard-landscaping elements complement one another beautifully and the planting-to-hard-landscape ratio is just right. The grey tones of the paving and wall panels provide a clean backdrop to the planting: yew topiary sited with restrained confidence. The middle section of the space is spanned by an impressive sheet of stone. In simple terms, this is a path, but a striking one that adds to the drama of the scheme. The slick, low-profile bench sits snugly among the topiary, as if it is an integral part of the landscaping. Its aluminium structure has a smooth, tactile finish and a precision engineering and alignment make it as good to sit on as to look at.

Lighting provides as much excitement as the initial reveal as you come through the front door. Shadows float across the walls, while stems of *Carpinus* (hornbeam) are accentuated with uplights, leading the eye systematically to the back of the garden and towards the entertaining area. Hidden strip lights bring the 'floating' stones to life to fascinating effect.

Right: A seamless transition between interior and exterior. Grey tones run throughout and contrast with the topiary blocks and the textures in the green wall.

VERDANT COURTYARD

Design Checklist

1. Use similar colour palettes and tones for the interior and exterior to create synergy and continuity. Muted grey materials in this instance give a clean, crisp feeling to the garden and make the evergreen planting really pop.

2. Pay attention to vertical elements in a small space as well as horizontal ones. Living walls soften the garden boundary, while horizontal cladding provides an enhanced and more focused perspective.

3. Zone a garden in order to create a versatile, multi-use space, with areas for entertaining, admiring and moving through. It should always be possible to explore a garden, even a small one – there is nothing more exciting for both children and adults.

4. Help a garden to look established by choosing semi-mature trees, and frame views within the space by lifting the crowns of trees to reveal clear stems. Multistemmed trees work well as architectural elements in their own right. Deciduous varieties often create a light canopy, which will cast dappled shadow, providing atmosphere and drama.

5. Introduce bold structure and evergreen interest with yew topiary. *Taxus* (yew) copes well in partial shade to full sun, as long as it has free-draining soil and enough water when it is getting established.

6. Use every available inch for planting. A thin strip of soil can provide a brilliant opportunity with the correct choice of plant. Here, underplanting the bench with ferns transforms an otherwise unused space.

7. Make the most of the available space by choosing custom-made furniture. Material choices are endless and so, too, are the detail decisions. Comfort must take priority; plan the angle of the backrest and the height of the seat to suit the users. This bench has a 19-degree pitch, with a seat height of 41cm (16in) – a happy medium between a dining and a lounge chair.

8. Choose attractive lighting for your garden, particularly if your property has a glass rear elevation and is on view all year round. You may not want to use the garden when it is cold and dark, but you should still be able to enjoy it.

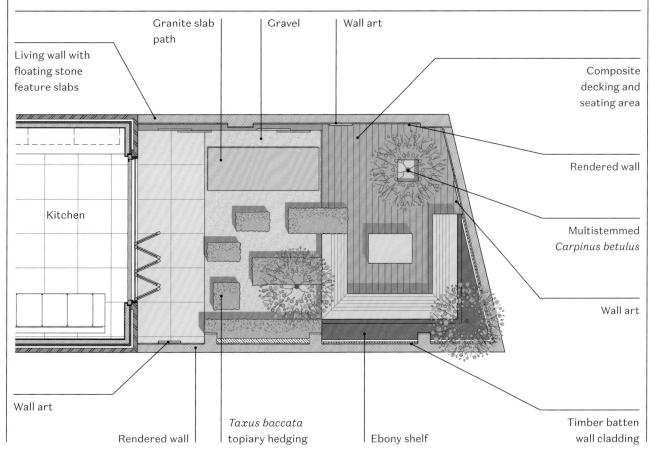

Living wall with floating stone feature slabs

Granite slab path

Gravel

Wall art

Composite decking and seating area

Rendered wall

Multistemmed *Carpinus betulus*

Wall art

Timber batten wall cladding

Kitchen

Wall art

Rendered wall

Taxus baccata topiary hedging

Ebony shelf

VERDANT COURTYARD

The Details

Floating stones are made possible with made-to-measure brackets.

Planted in bespoke aluminium tray planters, bun moss provides an injection of bright colour against the timber cladding. Much like the topiary, the moss-filled planters are repeated to enhance the restrained simplicity of the space.

Changes in level and vertical elements help to increase the sense of space.

Anodised aluminium furniture in the entertaining area.

Layered hedging of *Taxus baccata* (common yew) adds depth and drama.

Hidden strip lighting creates a floating effect.

A careful juxtaposition of materials forms effortless links.

Custom-made furniture makes effective use of available space.

Uplighting multistemmed trees adds atmosphere at night.

An underplanting of the vibrant green *Asplenium scolopendrium* (hart's tongue fern).

CASE STUDY

Pure Theatre

JO WILLEMS & JAN VAN OPSTAL

The designers of the famous gardens at De Heerenhof have theatre in their blood, as is evident from the wonderful way this garden in the suburbs of Maastrict, in the Netherlands, has been laid out to look like a stage set. Standing in the wings are tantalising green hummocks of clipped *Buxus* (box) that contrast with the strong, dark columns of *Taxus* (yew). But the garden hasn't even started yet. In spring, a cool, white ribbon of tulips and narcissi winds through the box spheres towards the pond, breaks at the clipped yew hedge and continues, much to your surprise, on the other side of the hedge and then on to and beyond the raised pond. This is the New Garden, built in 2002 by professional garden designers Jan van Opstal, a choreographer, and Jo Willems, a theatre director. It sits adjacent to their Old Garden, built some 30 years ago. Neither had gardened before they embarked on the Old Garden, which has the same mixture of formality and playfulness, while being more romantic and traditional than its new minimalist sister. Both gardens use a backbone of evergreen structure to stage areas, such as the double circle of box hedging that forms the Green Room in the Old Garden, where you want to pause and enjoy the scenery. Steel girders were used in the new garden to divide the area into rooms, framing the ever-changing views as you walk through. Both designers enjoy welcoming visitors, to which end they are always changing the scenery, moving pots, pruning trees and creating new plantings to tantalise and enchant.

Right: The view of the New Garden looking across the formal ponds to H' House, designed by Dutch architects Wiel Arets. Cloud-pruned box mounds contrast with the yew columns and tightly clipped yew hedge. Pleached apple trees soften the canopy.

PURE THEATRE

Design Checklist

1. Grow bulbs. They are incredibly versatile and, as well as being used in beds and pots, can be grown in lawns and meadows. To create a ribbon of bulbs, use a spade to cut away the turf in the shape you want to plant and then plant the bulbs, replacing the turf afterwards.

2. Naturalise bulbs in grass by throwing them across the ground and planting them where they fall. Use a hand trowel or bulb planter to plant them one by one. It is easier to plant after rain when the ground is not too hard.

3. Provide year-round structure. The New Garden at De Heerenhof is built around a permanent architecture of evergreen plants and steel that looks good all year.

4. Always buy good-quality bulbs from a specialist supplier who will usually have bulk offers. Check the bulbs are a good size and also firm, with no mould, and plant from mid to late autumn at a depth of twice the height of the bulb.

5. Grow better tulips. Most tulips will come up again after the first year, but are often smaller, which is why people buy fresh bulbs. Remove the flowering heads by pulling them off, but leave the foliage to die back naturally. If you plan to use the bulbs again, strengthen them after flowering by watering as needed and feeding once a week with a potassium-rich fertiliser until the leaves have died down.

6. Use containers to provide spots of colour. Again, bulbs are ideal for this, enabling you to change the mood of the garden each spring and summer. The 'Orange Emperor' tulips were planted by Jan van Opstal to mark the coronation of King Willem-Alexander of the Netherlands in 2013.

7. Enjoy yourself! It is very easy when embarking on a garden to be overwhelmed. Don't be afraid to do what you like and what you want. The very best gardens are reflections of their owners and will have a personality and spark.

8. Think of the garden as theatre and draw in your audience by preparing set pieces and surprises. The ribbon of tulips used here, for example, is a wonderful device, making you want to find out where it leads. Likewise, the Green Room in the Old Garden makes you stop to contemplate the scene.

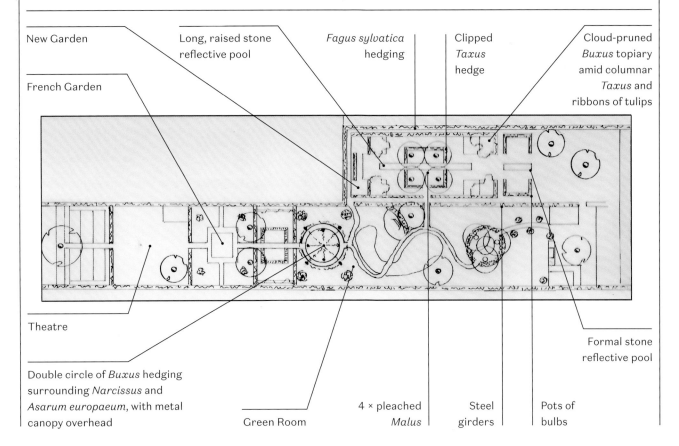

New Garden

French Garden

Long, raised stone reflective pool

Fagus sylvatica hedging

Clipped *Taxus* hedge

Cloud-pruned *Buxus* topiary amid columnar *Taxus* and ribbons of tulips

Theatre

Double circle of *Buxus* hedging surrounding *Narcissus* and *Asarum europaeum*, with metal canopy overhead

Green Room

4 × pleached *Malus*

Steel girders

Pots of bulbs

Formal stone reflective pool

PURE THEATRE

The Details

Steel girders play on the idea of garden rooms and interact with the green geometry to create a feeling of height and space.

Tulipa 'Orange Emperor' with deep purple pansies.

Ribbons of *Tulipa* 'Casablanca',
Narcissus 'Thalia', *N.* 'Ice Wings' and
Leucojum vernum (spring snowflake).

The ribbon of bulbs rolls on through
the box, across the lawn towards the
yew hedge and beyond.

Tulipa 'Ivory White' with white violas in
long metal planters.

The small formal pool outside the
house links the building with the
long raised pond.

Canalside Garden

CHARLOTTE ROWE

First impressions can be so deceiving. Looking out from the sub-basement kitchen of this house, you would never guess that this is a converted Victorian school on the side of a canal. Everything about the design seems so effortless, as the muted greys of the interior flow outside and up two flights of broad steps to a contemporary outdoor fireplace. This brilliantly breaks up the brutalism of the brick wall at the back of the space, which is 10m (33ft) tall.

The double-width garden can be seen from all three floors of the property, which has been fitted with dramatic double-height Crittall windows. The garden looks wonderful at night in the reflected red glow of the fire and illuminated by lights and lanterns in the trees.

The key to making this space breathe was to work with, and not against, the rather austere original structure and turn the difficulties posed by the two-level plot into an opportunity to create two separate seating areas that catch the sun at different times of the day. The morning sun falls on the lower level and by making the steps turn a corner the designers have created not only visual interest, but also a U-shaped eating area that is conveniently close to the kitchen for summer breakfasting. The shapes and colours of the kitchen furniture are echoed outdoors, doubling the impression of space. The planting softens the sharp edges of the architecture while also adding splashes of colour.

Left: Indoors and outdoors are seamlessly blended by extending the grey, polished poured concrete floors in the house outside into the garden. The darker grey gravel area, grey rendered walls and dark grey trellis provide a palette of colours that sets off the rich planting.

CANALSIDE GARDEN

Design Checklist

1. Use layers of green hedging to add depth and interest. In this garden, *Buxus sempervirens* (common box) and *Pleioblastus pygmaeus* (dwarf bamboo) have been chosen.

2. Add atmosphere and highlight dark corners with lighting. Easy and cheap, string lanterns or fairy lights in trees to show off their silhouettes and create feelings of height and depth. Solar-powered lighting is also useful, especially for tucked-away corners where you may not want to wire in permanent systems.

3. Complete a design with outdoor seating. The choice of furniture is key, so think hard about what you want it to achieve. Here, the bespoke seating continues the lines of the low walls, while easy chairs soften the area in front of the fire.

4. Keep colours simple. This is especially important in small spaces. In this instance, the colour palette is restricted to greys and greens with the only other accent coming from the contemporary orange cushions.

5. Enjoy your outdoor space in colder weather as well as through the summer by installing an attractive outdoor fire. The tall chimney breast at the heart of this design breaks up the monotony of the brick wall that would otherwise overwhelm this plot.

6. Get the contemporary look with gravel. The dark grey gravel used here gives the garden a modern feel and is easy to maintain, as well as providing a contrast in colour and texture against the smooth, pale grey of the surrounding walls and steps.

7. Install a trellis to provide privacy and soften it with evergreen climbers. Choose a trellis colour that blends in with the rest of the garden and that will ultimately disappear behind the mature planting.

8. Think about texture rather than just colour. In the upper bed a variety of textures is provided by a mixture of shrubs, grasses and perennials.

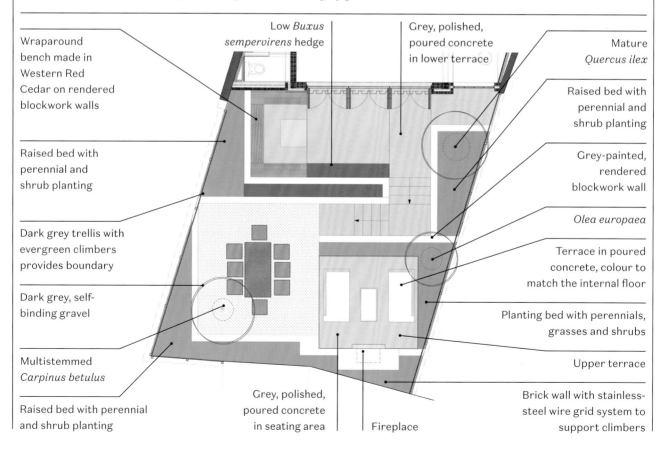

Wraparound bench made in Western Red Cedar on rendered blockwork walls

Raised bed with perennial and shrub planting

Dark grey trellis with evergreen climbers provides boundary

Dark grey, self-binding gravel

Multistemmed *Carpinus betulus*

Raised bed with perennial and shrub planting

Low *Buxus sempervirens* hedge

Grey, polished, poured concrete in seating area

Fireplace

Grey, polished, poured concrete in lower terrace

Mature *Quercus ilex*

Raised bed with perennial and shrub planting

Grey-painted, rendered blockwork wall

Olea europaea

Terrace in poured concrete, colour to match the internal floor

Planting bed with perennials, grasses and shrubs

Upper terrace

Brick wall with stainless-steel wire grid system to support climbers

Soften concrete edges with billowing evergreens.

Industrial-style dining seats echo the steel windows.

Summer colour is provided by *Agapanthus* 'Black Pantha' and a range of deep purple clematis.

Agapanthus 'Black Pantha' has wonderful deep blue, almost black, flowers and is very hardy but in extra-cold areas may need a thick winter mulch.

The Details

Wraparound seating catches the morning sun and provides a perfect spot for breakfast. The wide retaining walls double up as extra seating.

Multistemmed Carpinus betulus (common hornbeam) is a focal point.

Poured concrete flooring links indoors and out, and is best achieved with a flush threshold and no step down.

CASE STUDY

Overcoming Shade

SARA JANE ROTHWELL

This design shows how a minimal palette of materials and plants can create a wonderfully theatrical effect. The house itself is Arts and Crafts, but with a new brick extension, which includes floor-to-ceiling picture windows that open onto the garden. The back of the garden is heavily shaded by overhanging trees, but you'd never realise it as the design overrides this with strong horizontal bands of bright greens and reds. There is a lovely symmetry as you look from the kitchen to the soft grey, slatted hardwood bench set in the concrete walls of the water tank. The rusted Corten steel wall of the tank has been inset with five copper waterspouts that create a vertical display of constantly falling water. Planters on either side are filled with *Anemanthele lessoniana* (pheasant's tail grass) which gives colour and texture through the year. The tank is crested with a broad band of red *Persicaria affinis* 'Superba', a plant that is both striking and easy to maintain; this sets up the eye for the rising bands of lawn behind. Each grass step is banded with Corten steel risers and flanked by receding yew hedges. Finally, the eye comes to rest on the back wall with its panel of rusted steel and the grey slatted fence that mirrors the bench and water feature below. It's a brilliantly executed effect and hugely satisfying to look at. The genius of the design continues in a side patio and dining area where the greys are repeated in the polished floor and poured concrete walls. The gas firepit surrounds are finished with Corten steel. At night, underlit glass floor panels, wall lighting and the firepit illuminate the eating area.

Right: A clear geometry underpins this design. Looking from the house, a sense of space is created by the horizontal lines of the water feature topped with contrasting bands of the pink blooms and bright green foliage of *Persicaria*.

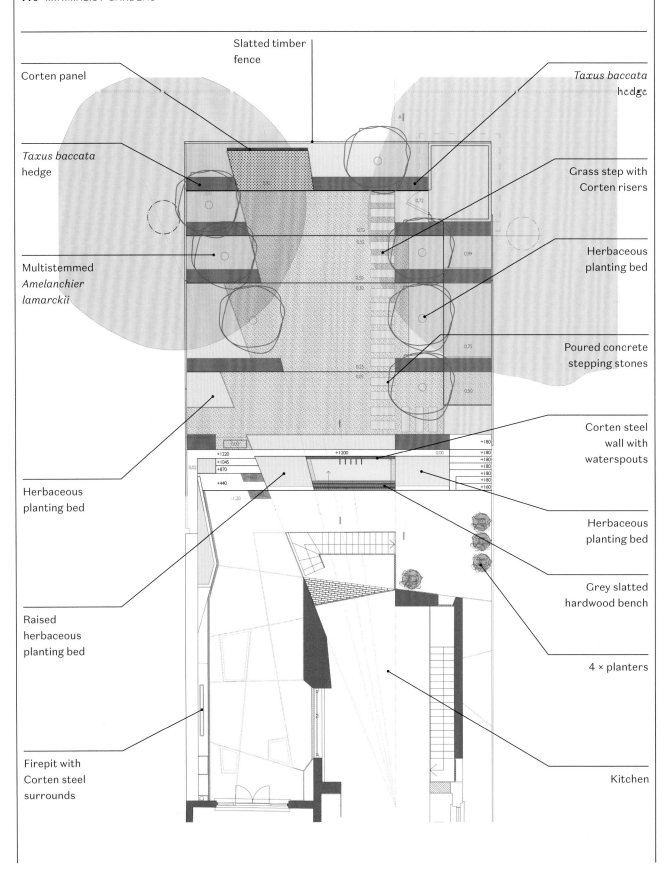

Slatted timber fence

Corten panel

Taxus baccata hedge

Taxus baccata hedge

Grass step with Corten risers

Multistemmed *Amelanchier lamarckii*

Herbaceous planting bed

Poured concrete stepping stones

Herbaceous planting bed

Corten steel wall with waterspouts

Herbaceous planting bed

Raised herbaceous planting bed

Grey slatted hardwood bench

Firepit with Corten steel surrounds

4 × planters

Kitchen

OVERCOMING SHADE

Design Checklist

1. Learn to manage dry shade.
This affects many town gardens. The best way round the problem is to grow shade-tolerant plants. In the heavily shaded upper area under the mature trees in this garden, cool white and fresh green planting lights up dark corners. The lawn has also been laid with a shade-tolerant grass mix.

2. Install instant warmth. Corten steel surrounds the wall firepit, which is set into the poured concrete walls. The owners can turn on the 1.8m- (6ft-) long gas burner with the flick of a switch. This is ideal for people who don't want to be bothered with logs and matches.

3. Think about the geometry of your space. This garden is focused on the kitchen, and one of the design briefs was to encourage the owners to spend more time outside. By using the lines of perspective the eye is naturally drawn towards the end of the garden.

4. Stick to a restrained palette for a powerful effect. This design has just three basic colours: the understated neutrals of the iroko hardwood and the poured concrete; the reds of the rusted steel and *Persicaria*; and the greens of the foliage, shrubs and grass.

5. Take the indoor aesthetic outside. In this garden, for example, the rusted Corten steel in the garden echoes the colours and materials of the sculptures inside the house. One area flows seamlessly into the other, enhancing the views in both directions.

6. Choose your seating carefully.
In this garden the pale and understated dining chairs and table chime with the minimal simplicity of the underlit glass floor panels and the slatted timbers of the iroko bench below the water feature, as well as the fence on the back wall.

7. Position features to block out unwanted views. In this garden, the rusted Corten steel panel feature has been deliberately placed against the back left wall so that it hides the top of the neighbour's shed.

8. Repeat planting to create impact.
The key plant here is *Persicaria affinis* 'Superba', an easy-going perennial with lovely, spiked flowerheads and bright green foliage. It is ideal to offset the rusted Corten steel and works well with the dark green of the yew hedges.

OVERCOMING SHADE

The Details

Persicaria affinis 'Superba' sprawls naturally over the poured concrete on top of the water feature.

Lighting features prominently in this garden, including wall-mounted fixtures and underlit glass floor panels.

Slatted iroko hardwood seating is both chic and hard-wearing.

Poured concrete stepping stones set into the lawn.

At night the underlit glass floor panels, gas firepit and wall lights add warmth to the view from the kitchen.

The planting bed is lined with a geotextile membrane and then filled with a layer of drainage material topped with lightweight soil. The utilitarian copper spouts (actually gas piping) will turn verdigris in time and stand out against the rusted steel.

The yew hedges are clipped into sharp 90-degree angles to emphasise the geometry of the garden.

Anemanthele lessoniana (pheasant's tail grass), shown in the foreground of this photo, looks good all year round.

CASE STUDY

A Rural Courtyard

SEAN WALTER

Two derelict dairies were linked with a contemporary extension to create a courtyard surrounded by a long, low modernist home. It is a striking design by the client, Simon Green of Moho London, with polished concrete floors and beams made from Douglas fir. The house stands in 16 hectares (40 acres), though only a fraction of those are actively gardened. Simon wanted to create a courtyard garden that worked with the minimalist architecture, as well as the setting, and brought in Sean Walter of The Plant Specialist to help with the design. Informal stone setts, laid in alternating linear blocks, are in keeping with the rural landscape and the buildings' original use, while also working with the brimming water feature and the sharp angles and lines of the house. At the heart of the design is an ancient eleagnus tree with a low-branching habit and silvery leaves. This has been framed with a bed edged with red Corten steel walls that pick up on the house's red brickwork. The eleagnus is underplanted with mounds of *Muehlenbeckia complexa* (Australian ivy), a small-leaved shrub with red tints in its wiry stems that echo the rusted steel. Another square bed has been planted with the hardy *Hakonechloa macra* (Japanese forest grass). The owner had wanted lawn in that area, but luckily Sean persuaded him of the benefits of the hakonechloa, which has sprays of small flowers in summer and turns russet in autumn, echoing the Corten steel-edged bed. As the cobblestone path moves away from the house, the change towards a more naturalistic feel in the area beyond is signalled by planting the crevices with flowering thyme.

Left: Looking from the contemporary new-build house, with its polished concrete floor, to the stone setts that echo the rural landscape. The massed mono plantings provide year-round architectural interest.

A RURAL COURTYARD

Design Checklist

1. Bring unity to a design with Corten steel. In this garden, Corten steel is used throughout for edging beds and on the steps down from the deck. The rusted iron picks up on the colour of the red bricks in the original farm buildings as well as the *Festuca rubra* (red fescue) in the meadow, the *Fagus sylvatica* f. *purpurea* (copper beech) in the garden and the red tints throughout the planting.

2. Incorporate existing plants. An old eleagnus has become the central focus of the courtyard. Its sprawling boughs have been framed by a raised Corten steel bed and it has been underplanted with *Muehlenbeckia complexa*, a wiry deciduous climbing plant whose red stems match the Corten steel edging.

3. Install a bespoke water feature. The pool in this garden was designed by Simon Green, the client, and is finished with Marbelite, a decorative plaster made from powdered marble mixed with cement. This is then highly polished so that, as the water spills over the edges of the square, it reflects and refracts light around the courtyard.

4. Employ natural stone setts or cobbles for either a traditional or modern design. Stones can be new or reclaimed. Those used here are made from reclaimed granite originally from the Liverpool docks. Setts are available in a variety of colours and sizes of granite, limestone, basalt, sandstone and porphyry.

5. Keep plants in pots happy by preparing containers well. Ensure there is good drainage by using a metal drill to add holes to the base of containers, if necessary (to avoid root rot). Line with broken crocks or pebbles before filling with good-quality potting compost.

6. Choose pots well. Large, Victorian, riveted, verdigris planters look perfect in this setting. The copper verdigris colouring is a great foil for plants.

7. Make a statement with massed mono plantings, which also work well with modern buildings. Choose evergreens for year-round colour or perennial grasses for a more airy effect.

8. Maintain containers. Automatic watering systems save time and ensure plants don't dry out. Water-retaining gel crystals can also be added. Each year, top pots with fresh compost and feed regularly in the growing season.

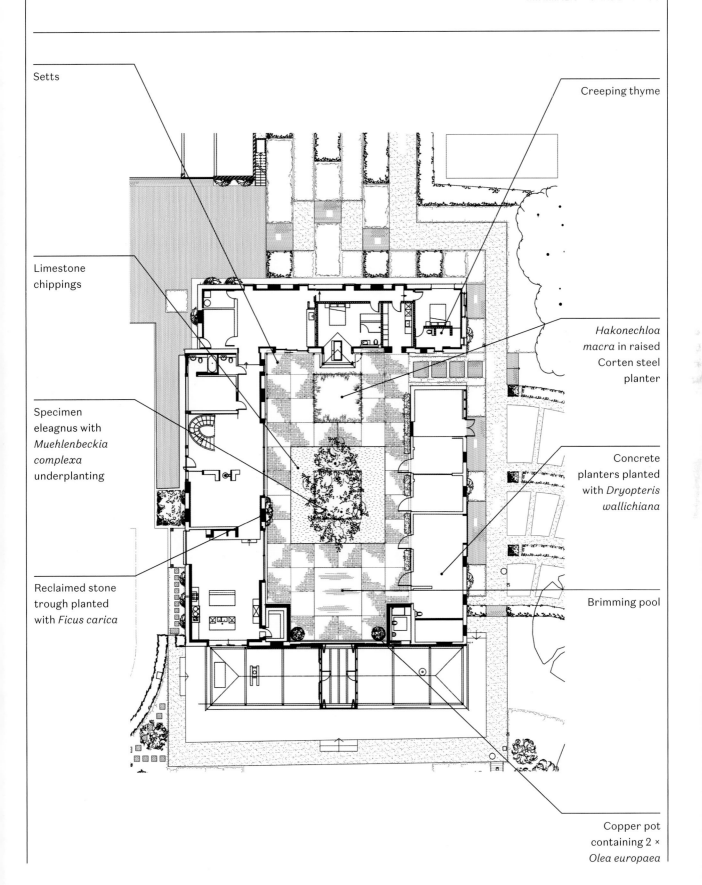

Setts

Creeping thyme

Limestone
chippings

*Hakonechloa
macra* in raised
Corten steel
planter

Specimen
eleagnus with
*Muehlenbeckia
complexa*
underplanting

Concrete
planters planted
with *Dryopteris
wallichiana*

Reclaimed stone
trough planted
with *Ficus carica*

Brimming pool

Copper pot
containing 2 ×
Olea europaea

The old elaeagnus in the Corten steel bed is underplanted with *Muehlenbeckia complexa* (Australian ivy).

Square beds of *Hakonechloa macra* (Japanese forest grass) contrast beautifully with the stone setts.

Two large concrete troughs designed by the client are abundantly planted with semi-evergreen *Dryopteris wallichiana* (alpine wood fern).

A reclaimed stone trough contains a fig, *Ficus carica*, with a bright green underplanting of *Soleirolia soleirolii* (mind-your-own-business).

The highly polished, brimming water feature lights up the courtyard with reflections. Using limestone chippings at the base avoids the harsh meeting of the Marbelite sides and the granite setts.

A RURAL COURTYARD

The Details

Reclaimed granite setts and grey limestone chippings (which tone with the polished concrete floor in the house) create a shadow gap around the water feature.

Planting crevices with thyme breaks up the path. Several varieties have been planted here, including *Thymus serpyllum* 'Pink Chintz'.

4

Plants First

CASE STUDY

Mediterranean Landscape

JAMES BASSON

This garden was created on the site of a newly built villa where there was a considerable amount of leftover rubble and rock. It was a tricky site and steeply sloped, but rather than fight against the prevailing conditions, the designer embraced the opportunities it provided. Some of the larger rocks were used to retain the slopes and create a rockery, while others were set aside to build steps into the hill so you can wander through the naturalistic planting. The site is hot and dry, but instead of importing lots of new topsoil, mulches and other soil improvers, plants were used that have adapted to cope with just such conditions. Mediterranean species are ideal for this as they thrive in poor soil where there is a lot of water runoff and very little irrigation. Cistus, lavender, rosemary and thyme were planted in their hundreds to provide ground cover and to soften the edges of steps and between rocks. Carpets of euphorbia and semi-evergreen *Atriplex halimus* (tree purslane) soften the hardscape and blend into the surrounding landscape of mature olive trees and local maquis.

The seating area consists of a kitchen and lounge area which is shaded by a pergola topped with reed screens that can be lifted off. A lovely wisteria twines around this, its large blooms picking up the dusty purples of the rosemary and sage flowers, while its gnarled trunk echoes those of the olives. The challenge was to integrate the oval-shaped swimming pool so it blended harmoniously with the rest of the garden and its surrounds. This was achieved by setting rocks close to the smooth pool paving and adding a small waterfall.

Right: The area between house and terrace is planted with dry-loving Mediterranean species, including *Coronilla valentina* subsp. *glauca* 'Citrina', *Atriplex halimus* and *Euphorbia characias*.

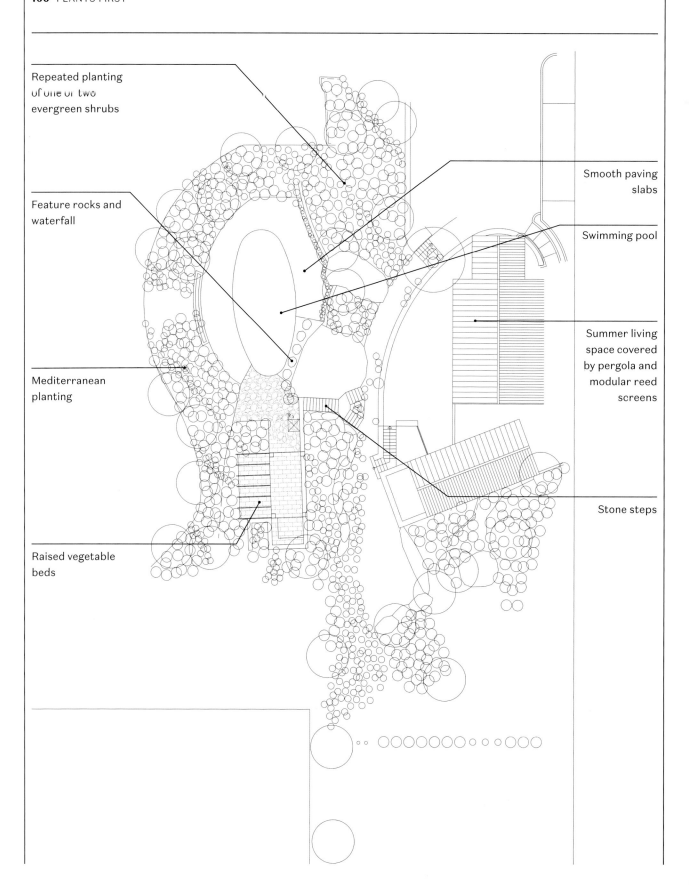

Repeated planting of one or two evergreen shrubs

Feature rocks and waterfall

Mediterranean planting

Raised vegetable beds

Smooth paving slabs

Swimming pool

Summer living space covered by pergola and modular reed screens

Stone steps

MEDITERRANEAN LANDSCAPE

Design Checklist

1. Use existing hard materials to minimise your carbon footprint and maximise the ways in which the garden blends into the local landscape. There was a lot of rubble and large rocks left on this site, so these were used to create rockscapes and steps, and also to retain the slopes.

2. Plant in poor soil and rubble to minimise weeds. Mediterranean plants are adapted to poor soil, so are ideal when planting any dry garden. Figs are a prime example of a plant that thrives on lack of care. If figs get too much moisture, they put all their energy into new shoots. Restrict them and they fight back by putting out fruits!

3. Allow your garden to flourish without watering by choosing a perfectly adapted plant palette and using the right plant in the right place. Mediterranean plants typically have spined or furry, silvery leaves and are happy in rough ground and gravel gardens. Cistus, lavender, rosemary, thyme and euphorbia are all ideal plants for such conditions.

4. Help integrate a swimming pool into the natural landscape by using local materials. Here, the rocks and stones left behind after the villa was built were placed around the smooth edge of the pool and make its shape feel less alien. But you could use whatever material suits your landscape.

5. Locate those parts of the garden that require hand-water close to the house. In this garden, the raised vegetable beds are situated directly behind the house.

6. Repeating one or two evergreen shrubs through the garden gives the feeling of a natural landscape, covers the ground all year and provides a strong base on which to hang the more decorative elements of the planting.

7. Consider modular reed screening. This can be moved around according to the season, all the while maintaining a rustic feel. In this garden, it is enhanced by a wisteria in spring and summer.

8. Think about the view. Make sure there are several places in your garden where you can sit and enjoy the view; here, for example, there is the poolside and summer outdoor lounge, as well as hidden secret spots within the planting.

MEDITERRANEAN LANDSCAPE

The
Details

The seating area is shaded by a screened canopy.
The modules of reed screen can be added or removed
as required. The pergola also supports a wisteria.

The soft palette of Mediterranean plants in shades of blue
and purple and a glaucous greeny grey is perfectly offset
by the muted turquoise paint on the wooden shutters.

The stone steps are softened with gently mounding *Atriplex halimus* (tree purslane) and acid-green torches of euphorbia.

Plantings of thyme look entirely naturalised growing between the rocks, just as they do in the surrounding maquis.

Steely purple-grey spires of lavender. Three different varieties were used across the garden. Snip the stems after flowering, cutting down to 2.5cm (1in) above the woody growth.

CASE STUDY

Hope on the Horizon

MATT KEIGHTLEY

A garden with meaning and message, this was my first show garden at RHS Chelsea Flower Show and I drew inspiration for the space from my younger brother Michael's experience of the conflict in Afghanistan as a serving soldier. As well as raising awareness of the support Help for Heroes provides for service personnel, I wanted the garden to be a place for relaxation and solace; somewhere for reflection where people could forget their cares and worries. The title 'Hope on the Horizon' was the effect I wanted it to have on those who would use the garden.

A clear path runs through the garden, framed by totems of *Carpinus* (hornbeam) and directing the focus towards the sculpture set within the rear boundary hedge. Granite blocks (representing physical health) begin in rough, raw and natural form and become more and more refined through the garden. Planting goes through a similar transition and represents psychological wellbeing, starting with pockets of intense colour and gradually becoming more calm and serene.

Blocks of *Buxus* (box) pull the scheme together, subtly adjusting the levels and perspective and accenting the blocks of granite. The very structured approach is diluted by drifts of perennial colour that snake around the garden, leading the eye to yet more unexpected excitement. The heavily clipped *Taxus* (yew) hedge forms the perfect boundary and partition lines. Like an interior space I compartmentalised the garden, to offer multiple opportunities for escapism and secluded rest.

Left: The 'Hope on the Horizon' garden was relocated to Chavasse VC House, in Colchester, a centre set up to help recovering servicemen and women.

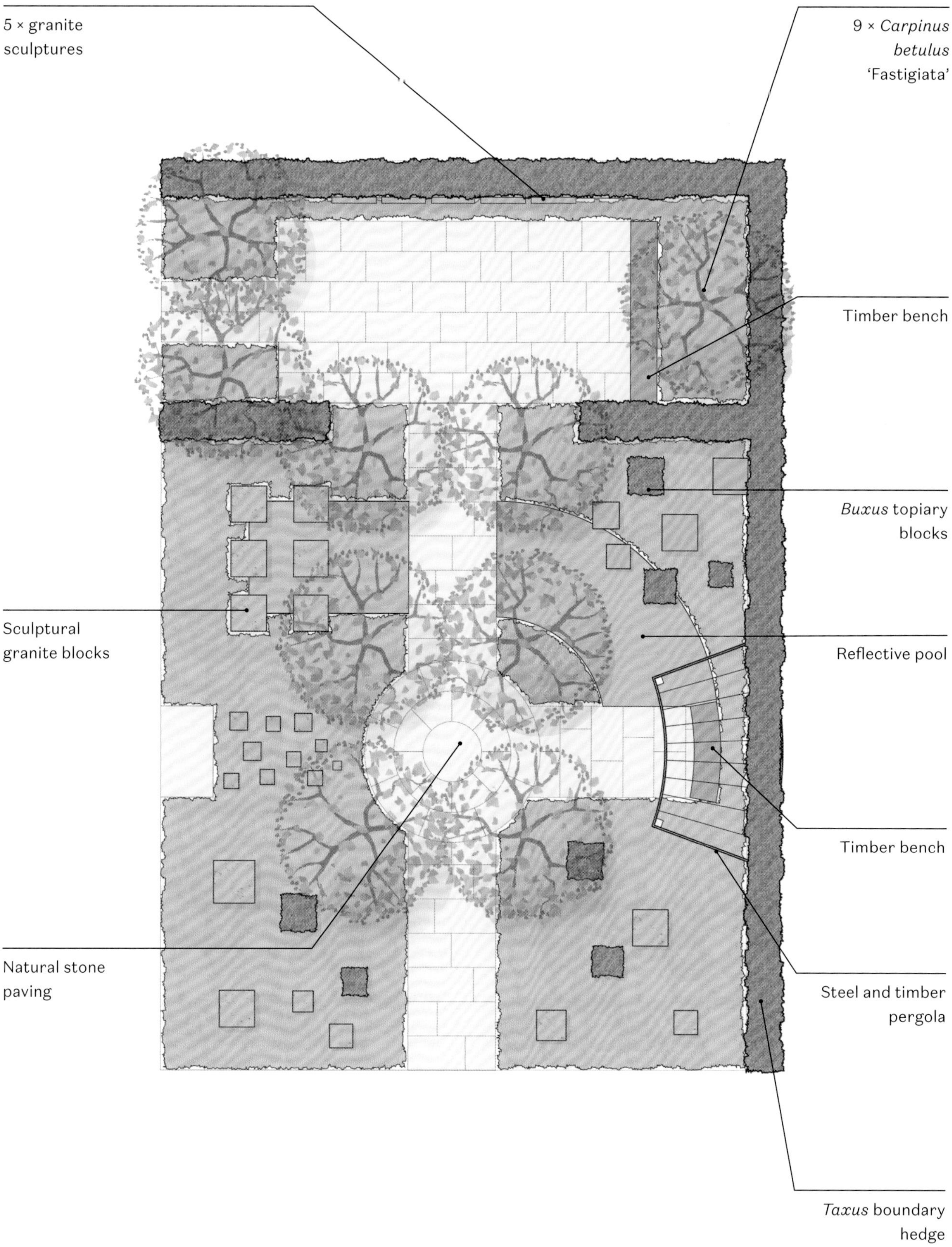

5 × granite
sculptures

9 × *Carpinus
betulus*
'Fastigiata'

Timber bench

Buxus topiary
blocks

Sculptural
granite blocks

Reflective pool

Timber bench

Natural stone
paving

Steel and timber
pergola

Taxus boundary
hedge

HOPE ON THE HORIZON

Design Checklist

1. Use focal points to draw the view through a space and provide thought-provoking points of interest. It is vital to establish how the focal points are framed and thus perceived. In this case, the 'rim' on the rear boundary was framed by *Carpinus* (hornbeam) in an attempt to achieve an intense focus.

2. Create movement, layers and depth within a scheme – even in the tightest of spots – by introducing undulation. Start with ground cover and low-growing species and build the scheme up with multiple heights. Plant the structural elements and then consider how perennials can drift through them.

3. Set the tone of a garden and provide a backdrop for the planting through your choice of material colours. Warm honey or oat tones give a subtle and welcoming feel, while a more muted grey palette can appear contemporary (although sometimes cold in the wrong environment).

4. Add structure and height using trees. In more confined spaces, I advise opting for a deciduous specimen to ensure the leaf cover doesn't block out too much light in the colder months when the sun is lower.

5. Add excitement with water, whether it's moving, still or used for the relaxing sound it makes. There is something enchanting about a mirror pool – the reflections give you a greater appreciation of the surrounding garden and the wider landscape. The unknown depth is mesmerising and encourages visitors to pause and look.

6. Divide the space. Don't give away the garden in the first few steps. Create interesting divisions with hard landscaping, hedges, planting or a clever layout of paths.

7. Plant avenues in your garden. With the right tree, this is possible even in small to medium gardens. *Carpinus*, which can withstand hard pruning, is ideal and creates great topiary.

8. Create a calm space by integrating colour with subtlety and using gentle hues that blend into each other. Pockets can be planted more intensively, as long as the edges are softened by easing individual plants into the wider scheme.

Sunlight filters through the canopies of *Carpinus betula* 'Fastigiata' and catches the grasses above the structural plants.

A pocket of shade-loving plants enjoys the shelter of the trees.

Swaths of the catmint *Nepeta racemosa* 'Walker's Low' drift between blocks of granite and *Buxus* (box) that lead the eye through the garden.

Herbs complement the colours and tones in the perennial scheme and bring scent to the fringes of paths.

Solid blocks of granite nestled among the planting represent the soldiers' physical wellbeing at particular stages of the recovery process.

'Rim', a striking sculpture by Mary Bourne, depicts the horizon, creating a focus for the soldiers who eventually used the garden.

The Details

Lupinus 'Red Rum' adds vertical structure and vivid magenta to the scheme and is used as a metaphor for the distress felt at the start of recovery.

An avenue of *Carpinus betula* 'Fastigiata' stands tall and flanks the main path through the garden, creating a cathedral-like effect.

CASE STUDY

Contemporary Woodland

DECLAN BUCKLEY

This garden provides a brilliant solution to the eternal problem of what to do with a small shady patch. The typical scenario is a dense canopy of mature trees that eclipse the light, destroying any residual lawn, while the root-filled soil is so dry that little will grow. Here, the designer has turned the situation from disaster to triumph, creating a magical woodland that can be seen from all sides of the sleek modern house with its walls of floor-to-ceiling sliding glass and sunny roof terrace. As nearly all the plants are evergreen, this garden looks verdant all year round. It is not a large space, but manages to enchant because the smooth paths (which double up as a tricycle track for the clients' young daughter) draw you into the heart of the woodland. This is underplanted with a mass of bulbs that spark into life before the mature oak and lime trees come into leaf. There's a simplicity to the planting that echoes the minimalism of the house, while the smooth-edged paths and beds both contain and contrast with the carpets of grasses and ferns. Multistemmed shrubs grow like miniature trees above mass plantings of evergreen ferns, perennials and *Hakonechloa macra* (Japanese forest grass), creating the impression of a mature woodland in miniature. The original trees were pruned to provide strong silhouettes all year round. In time the overly dominant brickwork will be lost behind evergreen climbers, while rusted Corten steel tanks and contemporary furniture complete the look.

Right: All the plants here are happy under the canopy of the mature oak and lime trees and offer great variety of leaf colour, shape and texture. As the garden needs to perform all year, flowering plants have been selected for their long flowering period.

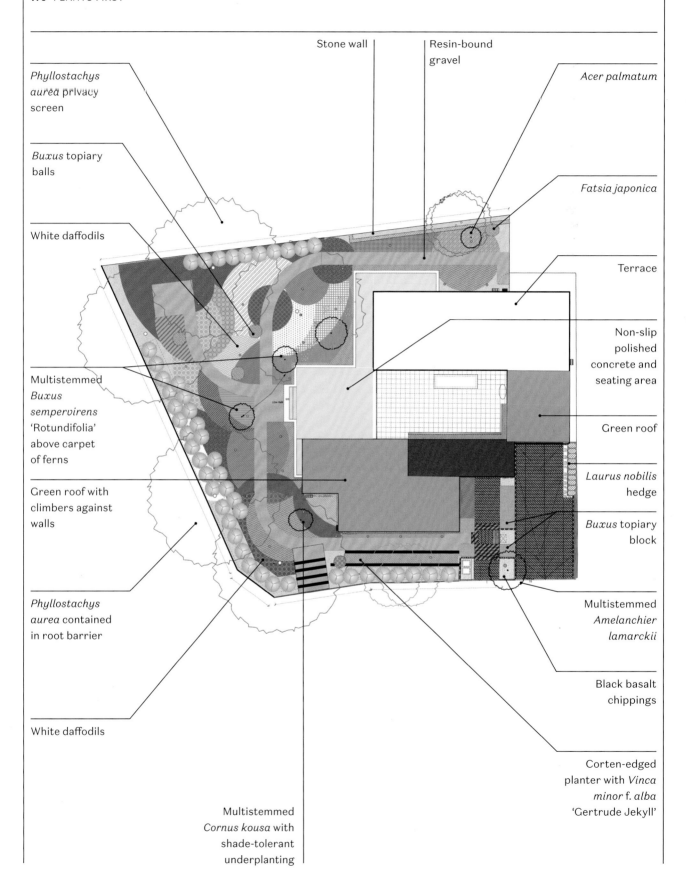

Phyllostachys
aurea privacy
screen

Buxus topiary
balls

White daffodils

Multistemmed
*Buxus
sempervirens*
'Rotundifolia'
above carpet
of ferns

Green roof with
climbers against
walls

*Phyllostachys
aurea* contained
in root barrier

White daffodils

Stone wall

Resin-bound
gravel

Multistemmed
Cornus kousa with
shade-tolerant
underplanting

Acer palmatum

Fatsia japonica

Terrace

Non-slip
polished
concrete and
seating area

Green roof

Laurus nobilis
hedge

Buxus topiary
block

Multistemmed
*Amelanchier
lamarckii*

Black basalt
chippings

Corten-edged
planter with *Vinca
minor* f. *alba*
'Gertrude Jekyll'

CONTEMPORARY WOODLAND

Design Checklist

1. Provide low-maintenance, year-round foliage using evergreen perennials. Good specimens include *Disporopsis* (large, leathery leaves), *Liriope* (sword-shaped leaves and blue flowers), *Epimedium* (beautiful, heart-shaped foliage), *Euphorbia* (strongly upright with acid-green bracts), *Vinca minor* (common periwinkle) and ferns.

2. Partner non-slip polished concrete with contemporary architecture. Match the proportions of the building to give the impression that the garden is an extension of the house. Here, the original sunken terrace was simply resurfaced so that it now feels like an extension of the house.

3. Opt for Corten steel for a modern yet natural effect. The rusted-steel colour of this popular contemporary material works remarkably well with fresh green foliage and, in winter, the strong shapes will provide your garden with much-needed structure.

4. Choose resin-bound gravel with steel edges for paths. It has a clean finish and is ideal for creating sweeping curves. It is permeable, offers good grip and can be easily maintained.

5. Recognise the value of hardy evergreen shrubs in small gardens. Here, scented *Osmanthus × burkwoodii*, *Aucuba japonica* f. *longifolia* 'Salicifolia' (Japanese laurel), and *Skimmia × confusa* 'Kew Green' are used.

6. Don't be afraid to tackle overly dominant trees and shrubs. A small garden is easily overwhelmed by large trees, but an experienced tree surgeon will know how to achieve the best results – for both the trees and your plot. Always consult an expert if undertaking any serious remedial work.

7. Think big – mass plantings achieve powerful effects. In this garden, several hundred ferns were planted to create a green carpet. It takes confidence to limit yourself to a single species, but the results are worth it.

8. Don't forget spring bulbs. You cannot see them at the moment in this garden, but in spring the woodland erupts with colour. There are bulbs for every location and they can be planted in beds, under trees and along banks. Try *Galanthus* (snowdrops), scillas, tulips, allium and crocus, for example.

CONTEMPORARY WOODLAND

The Details

Pots of succulents create instant effects in sunny spots. The plants will soon tumble attractively over the edge.

Hakenochloa macra (Japanese forest grass) is a deciduous perennial grass with airy green flowers in summer. The leaves turn reddish brown in autumn and last into winter.

The handmade statement furniture for indoors and out is crafted from basalt fibre, which is strong and light. The pieces of furniture are finished with a marine-grade polyurethane gel-coat for lifetime protection.

The multistemmed box, *Buxus sempervirens* 'Rotundifolia', and *Cornus kousa* rise above the carpet of ferns to create a dense woodland feel.

The choice of furniture is as important outdoors as it is indoors. Here, the minimalist sunlounger works well on the sunny roof terrace with the rusted Corten steel planter.

A leaf of *Polystichum setiferum* Proliferum Group. The evergreen fern *P. braunii* (Braun's holly fern) also features in this garden.

A shade-tolerant mixed planting with a variety of leaf shapes, including the small, groundcovering *Persicaria affinis* 'Darjeeling Red' with its pale flower spikes in the foreground.

Libertia grandiflora has creamy flowers that contrast with the box mounds and *Phyllostachys aurea* bamboo screen.

Texture and Form

JANE BROCKBANK

The owner of this garden, John Smart of John Smart Architects, had already put up the distinctive steel and rusted steel timber screen that forms one boundary wall when he brought in garden designer Jane Brockbank to collaborate on creating a garden. As an architect he was interested in texture and form, and in using these to inform both the hard landscaping and the planting. The end result is a design that is strikingly contemporary and yet filled with delicate planting. Outside the house, slim silver birches screen the road with their lacy foliage and provide the focus for a verdant woodland understorey. This sits against the patterned background of the scalloped terracotta wall tiles, which were saved from the old coach house that previously stood on the site. The paths and paving throughout are made from Danish brick in slightly different sizes and varying tones of grey to give a naturalistic feel. In the back garden, the oak table and benches stand on an island of grey brick surrounded by a sea of gravel into which are sown drifts of perennials and grasses. The scheme is mainly greens with hummocks of *Sesleria autumnalis* (autumn moor-grass) and highlights of purples and pinks from *Digitalis* (foxgloves), rodgersia and low-growing *Lamium* (dead nettle) and *Trifolium* (clover). In the front garden, the theme continues with rivers of *Luzula nivea* (snow rush) either side of the path and alternately planted *Euphorbia amygdaloides* var. *robbiae* and the froth of the pink cow parsley, *Chaerophyllum hirsutum* 'Roseum'.

Left: The owner wanted a planting scheme that focused on texture, form and pattern rather than colour. Jane Brockbank's planting of softly textured grasses and perennials in the island beds complements the more formal lines of the hard landscaping.

TEXTURE AND FORM

Design Checklist

1. Create maximum impact in a small space with a low-maintenance gravel garden. In this garden the edge-of-woodland, semi-shade plants appear to be growing through the gravel, but each island bed is in fact edged with metal.

2. Employ texture in your garden. Pattern and texture are as important as colour, but so often overlooked. Think about texture in the hard landscaping, perhaps contrasting smooth with rough. Try using cobbles and gravel, and juxtaposing hard landscaping with softly exuberant planting.

3. Plant a living screen. *Betula albosinensis* (Chinese birch), with its white stems, creates an effective screen, here hiding the house from the road. The white-bloomed bark peels to a rich red-brown and the leaves turn yellow in autumn.

4. Light from below. Soft under-lighting creates a subtle mood. Red LED lights placed below the concrete benches diffuse the light and draw the eye to the feature wall and the display of terracotta pots.

5. Offset paving stones to create an informal border that blurs the boundaries. The Danish Petersen bricks used here come in a range of sizes and varying tones of grey. Fine gravel between the paving and bed allows for some self-seeding.

6. Stick to a colour theme. Green is the unifying colour in the planting combinations here, with accents of deep purples and dusty, pinky browns that pick up on the rusted steel on the fence and the warm tones of the terracotta pots and oak furniture.

7. Paint fencing to set it into the background. The wooden fence here is painted in Mouse's Back from Farrow & Ball.

8. Make a statement wall. The screen wall in the back garden has been lifted out of the ordinary by incorporating subtly coloured, rusted steel uprights and diagonals.

9. Place small, clump-forming plants beside a path. Here, these include *Lamium maculatum* 'Beacon Silver' (dead nettle), *Acaena microphylla* 'Kupferteppich' and *Saxifraga × urbium* (London Pride), with pretty pink flowers.

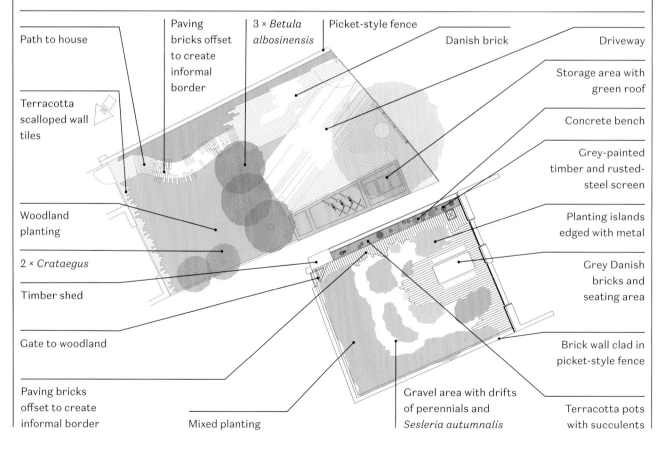

Path to house

Terracotta scalloped wall tiles

Woodland planting

2 × *Crataegus*

Timber shed

Gate to woodland

Paving bricks offset to create informal border

Paving bricks offset to create informal border

3 × *Betula albosinensis*

Picket-style fence

Mixed planting

Gravel area with drifts of perennials and *Sesleria autumnalis*

Danish brick

Driveway

Storage area with green roof

Concrete bench

Grey-painted timber and rusted-steel screen

Planting islands edged with metal

Grey Danish bricks and seating area

Brick wall clad in picket-style fence

Terracotta pots with succulents

Foxgloves and rodgersia add strong uprights among low-growing
Acaena microphylla 'Kupferteppich' and the orange highlights
of *Papaver atlanticum* (Atlas poppy) behind the oak furniture.

Ferns provide the perfect natural foil for the formal uprights of the timber screen.

TEXTURE AND FORM

The Details

The path leading to the side gate is edged with acid-green clumps of *Alchemilla erythropoda* (dwarf lady's mantle).

The warm tones of the rusted steel uprights are picked up by the terracotta pots arranged on the bespoke concrete benches.

Purple flowerheads of *Trifolium repens* 'William' grow through the acid-green of *Euphorbia seguieriana* subsp. *niciciana*.

Ferns, luzula and the tall red thistle *Cirsium rivulare* spill over the edging of Danish pavers.

CASE STUDY

City Shade

SEAN WALTER

Shade is almost inevitable in a city garden and is often greeted with dismay, but as this garden shows there are solutions. The planting is as dramatic and inventive as can be. The secret is, as ever, to embrace the conditions and work with what you have. Sean Walter of The Plant Specialist came up with a design that has form and structure while also allowing for a more billowing expressiveness that offsets and partially disguises the stern brick walls and other parts of the hard landscaping. The garden is divided into four levels – the studio garden level, the seating/dining area, a large metal balcony and a basement alley that wraps round the house. A multistemmed *Osmanthus × fortunei* stands at the heart of a green sea of *Hakonechloa macra* (Japanese forest grass), helping to create a visual break between the house and the studio. In autumn this produces scented white flowers, while the hakonechloa is interspersed with *Astrantia* 'Buckland', *Geranium macrorrhizum* 'Alba' and *Tulipa* 'Ballerina' for spring interest. This tulip, with its orange, lily-shaped flowers that gleam in low light, is one of the very few scented tulips. At night, uplighters show up the Japanese lines of the pruned osmanthus stems. Steps from this area lead up to more seating on the balcony. The metal railings on either side of these are hidden under the climbing tendrils of the shade-tolerant purple *Clematis* 'Étoile Violette'. The owner, Charlotte Crosland, is an interior designer and her hand is evident in the clean lines of the furniture, the stone-topped table and the stone sphere that mirrors the green globes of *Buxus* (box).

Left: A pair of white flowering cherry trees, *Prunus* 'Umineko', reach across the steps that lead from the balcony to the dining area. The heads of white hydrangeas light up the shade while adding to the woodland atmosphere.

CITY SHADE

Design Checklist

1. Unify the hard landscaping. The house walls are of warm London stock brick, which has been matched with reclaimed York stone. York flagstones are used in the eating area and York setts in the garden outside the studio.

2. Underplant to make a difference. *Buxus* (box) is used to hide the bare stems of taller herbaceous perennials. (The bed is too narrow for softer, lower planting.) The effect of underplanting the amelanchier with *Melica*, hellebores and ferns is a softer woodland feel.

3. Light up the dark with whites. The globe-shaped flowerheads of hydrangea work hard to light up the terrace. Other whites in this garden include *Rosa* 'Iceberg' and the stalwart *Anemone × hybrida* 'Honorine Jobert', not to mention the white blossom of the cherries and amelanchiers in spring.

4. Add character via multistemmed trees. Tree nurseries prune many tree varieties to create an open vase shape with several stems; these work well as single specimens. They are invaluable in small spaces, especially for their winter silhouettes. Here, multistemmed amelanchiers are planted in each corner of the small studio garden.

5. Choose plants with different tones. There are many shades of green. Walk through a wood and you see a range of greens, from the bright green of young oaks to the near-black needles of yew. Celebrate this green tapestry.

6. Make use of repetition. Three identical terracotta pots planted with hostas make a statement whereas one would not. Use this technique to provide instant impact, remembering that odd numbers are usually more satisfying to look at than even ones, so make groups of threes and fives.

7. Make the most of leaf shapes. Textures and details show up well in shade. Consider contrasting flat, palmate leaves with strappy leaves; grasses with heart-shaped leaves; and small against large.

8. Choose the right ground cover. The box hedge edging the beds in the eating area is rimmed with *Soleirolia soleirolii* (mind-your-own-business), which thrives in shade, making it an invaluable ground cover. However, this is highly invasive and needs to be restrained with hard landscaping or it can spread through beds and lawns.

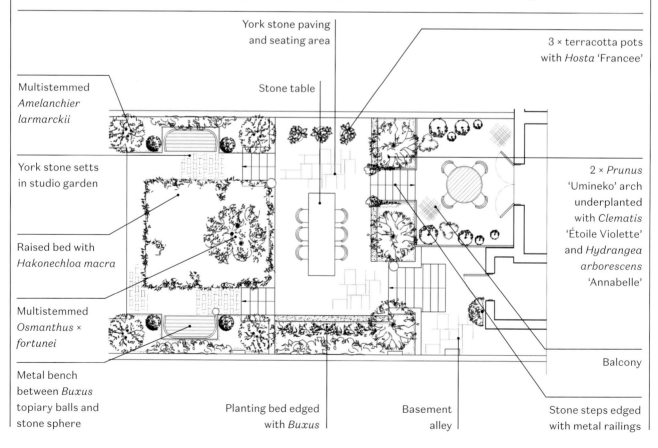

Multistemmed *Amelanchier larmarckii*

York stone setts in studio garden

Raised bed with *Hakonechloa macra*

Multistemmed *Osmanthus × fortunei*

Metal bench between *Buxus* topiary balls and stone sphere

York stone paving and seating area

Stone table

Planting bed edged with *Buxus*

Basement alley

3 × terracotta pots with *Hosta* 'Francee'

2 × *Prunus* 'Umineko' arch underplanted with *Clematis* 'Étoile Violette' and *Hydrangea arborescens* 'Annabelle'

Balcony

Stone steps edged with metal railings

A row of traditional terracotta pots abundantly planted with the plantain lily, *Hosta* 'Francee'.

As it weathers, the cut-metal lantern will rust and blend in with the planting.

An underplanting of ferns, rodgersia and grass beneath a multistemmed *Amelanchier lamarckii* (snowy mespilus).

Steps down from the balcony lead to the dining area with the osmanthus in the background.

The lantern (with *Hydrangea arborescens* 'Annabelle' in the background) echoes the shape of the dining chair backs.

Hakonechloa macra (Japanese forest grass) and *Astrantia* 'Buckland' with *Hosta* 'Francee' in the background.

The Details

Shade-tolerant *Clematis* 'Étoile Violette' climbs over the metal railings, bordered by the large, white flowerheads of *Hydrangea arborescens* 'Annabelle'.

Reclaimed York stone setts edged with *Hakonechloa macra* (Japanese forest grass) and offset by *Buxus* (box) globes.

CASE STUDY

An Urban Villa

TOM STUART-SMITH

The garden of this Regency villa in London is unusual in having two very contrasting spaces. The area at the side of the house is relatively private but, being built over an underground swimming pool, has no depth of soil, so much of the planting has to be in containers. Fortunately, the areas in between the supporting roof beams of the pool are deep enough to allow for some small, shallow-rooted trees. But with no space for deep-rooted trees in this secluded side garden, the designer, Tom Stuart-Smith, opted for seven mature olive trees in large terracotta pots, spilling over with thyme and erigeron. The garden that fronts onto the busy street has a little more depth of soil but has been designed with the intention of it being viewed from the upper floors of the house and is quietly theatrical. It is tightly composed and built up with many levels. Layers of pleached limes and yew hedges create a strong structural backdrop for looser planting so that there is a constant and deeply satisfying contrast of textures. A gate links this space to the quieter, more secluded garden at the side of the house, which contains some of the same plants.

Right: The garden fronting onto the street has been designed to be looked at from the house. It is highly structured using finely calibrated textures to create interest. The more static background of pleached limes and yew hedges contrasts with the looser form of *Cornus kousa* and the strappy *Hakonechloa macra* in the foreground. To the left of the picture is one of the owner's beehives.

AN URBAN VILLA

Design Checklist

1. Include evergreen structure. A framework of dramatic structural evergreens in the side garden provides year-round form and interest.

2. Add height. Climbers play a key role in a small space. In the side garden, the plants include *Wisteria sinensis*, *Trachelospermum jasminoides*, *Clematis* 'Huldine', *Rosa × odorata* 'Mutabilis', the yellow climber *R.* 'Alister Stella Gray', the rambling, creamy white, highly fragrant *R.* 'Aimée Vibert', *Hydrangea petiolaris* and the blue *Convovulus sabatius*.

3. Use shrubs to your advantage. Every garden benefits from a backbone of shrubs. The side garden contains *Pittosporum tobira*, *Eriobotrya japonica* (which has the advantage of shallow roots and produces little apricot loquats), *Laurus nobilis angustifolia* and *Magnolia grandiflora*.

4. Make use of symmetry – or not. Tom Stuart-Smith is wary of creating perfect symmetry as it is never found in nature. If you study the designs of both these gardens you will notice that, while there is a wonderful balance and harmonious repetition, everything always strays just a little off the beat.

5. Select the right furniture. The furniture in this garden is deliberately ornate and slightly tongue in cheek. In such a highly composed garden, stripped-back slick contemporary seating would have been too much. Instead, the designer has undercut the

formal design and injected a gentle touch of humour with gloriously over-the-top Baroque chairs.

6. Use planting to link the spaces. As the designer has done in this garden, two distinct spaces can be woven together through consistency of planting.

7. Place plants with care. The cloud-clipped box hedge in the garden fronting the street is created from around 50 box spheres of varying diameters. The spheres seem randomly placed but each was positioned exactly so as to avoid creating any observable pattern.

8. Underplant. In the side garden *Daphne bholua* 'Alba', *Cornus kousa* and *Gleditsia triacanthos* are underplanted with *Astrantia major* 'Ruby Wedding', *Helleborus orientalis*, hakonechloa and *Asarum europaeum*, which is a useful ground cover.

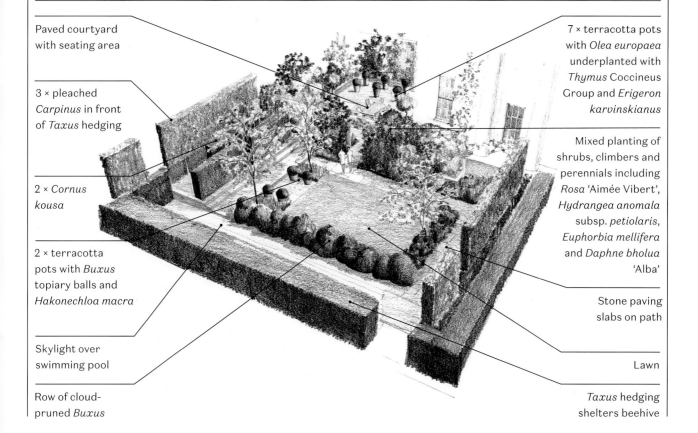

Paved courtyard with seating area

3 × pleached *Carpinus* in front of *Taxus* hedging

2 × *Cornus kousa*

2 × terracotta pots with *Buxus* topiary balls and *Hakonechloa macra*

Skylight over swimming pool

Row of cloud-pruned *Buxus*

7 × terracotta pots with *Olea europaea* underplanted with *Thymus* Coccineus Group and *Erigeron karvinskianus*

Mixed planting of shrubs, climbers and perennials including *Rosa* 'Aimée Vibert', *Hydrangea anomala* subsp. *petiolaris*, *Euphorbia mellifera* and *Daphne bholua* 'Alba'

Stone paving slabs on path

Lawn

Taxus hedging shelters beehive

AN URBAN VILLA

The
Details

Cornus kousa has clusters of tiny flowers surrounded by large white oval bracts. In autumn, deep pink fruit clusters are accompanied by reddish purple foliage.

The teak Blanchard chairs, in the style of Louis XV, come from Belgium and are designed to be used outdoors. The accompanying table can be made bespoke.

A play of loose and easy textures, with the oval *Cornus kousa* leaves contrasting with the strappy grass.

Clipped box globes in pots can be moved to the desired position. Again, this is all about contrasting textures and forms from the smooth lawn, the flowing grasses and the neat box spheres.

Softly billowing plants almost create a green bower around the gate to the side garden.

A formal line of pleached limes stands in front of yew hedges with soft green underplanting.

Large terracotta pots planted with mature olive trees and underplanted with *Thymus* Coccineus Group and *Erigeron karvinskianus*. Even in a city, large terracotta pots like these will need tying to the floor or to a nearby building to stop them being blown over in high winds.

CASE STUDY

Interconnecting Areas

SEAN WALTER

First impressions here suggest a garden with open spaces and a wealth of seating choices. A garden, then, that is surely much larger than the actual area of 20sq m (215sq ft) outside the L-shaped London home of textile designer Neisha Crosland. So how was this relatively small space made to appear so generous? The answer lies in the way it has been broken up into different zones, each enclosed with high walls and each with its own distinct character. Reclaimed York stone setts and slight changes in level help to define these different areas. Not an inch has been wasted, with walls trained with climbers and trees underplanted, while the terraces are given structure with collections of planted containers. Ugly gas meters are housed inside a wooden cupboard that now supports an ever-changing theatre of planted-up pots, while the air-conditioning unit has been disguised behind a water feature. Who would ever guess that the vertical wall of *Muehlenbeckia* through which a narrow spout pours into a brimming stone dish isn't just there for show? To complete the deceit, either side is framed with stones into which one of Neisha's designs has been lightly etched. London stock brick is complemented by the warm York stone flags and setts so that each area feels part of an interlinked whole, while topiaried *Quercus ilex* (holm oak) and silver-leaved olives lend height. A genius touch is arranging nine galvanized planters in a three-by-three grid, which gives architectural form as well as somewhere for planting.

Right: Formal topiary in the form of six holm oaks and low clipped box provides neat structure in this city garden.
By breaking up the space into a lawn, terraces and edged beds, the garden appears much bigger than it actually is.

INTERCONNECTING AREAS

Design Checklist

1. Multipy for offoot. In this garden, nine identical galvanized planters are arranged in a grid of three rows to create a statement on the cobbled patio. These planters contain spring bulbs that are followed by herbs, peppers and tomatoes in summer.

2. Maximize the feeling of space by dividing up a plot. Breaking up an area into several smaller ones gives the impression that more is going on and allows you to create different moods and atmospheres.

3. Create instant impact that keeps working all year round with topiary evergreen trees. Here, six *Quercus ilex* (holm oak) add structure and stature to help balance the height of the building.

4. Hide unsightly features such as the gas meter, which has been covered by wooden-fronted cupboards that are now used to display an ever-changing collection of stone pots in complementary shapes and sizes. And who would guess that the water feature conceals the air-conditioning unit?

5. Underplant, underplant, underplant. Not planting the ground beneath a tree just wastes a garden's potential. Here, Sean Walter underplanted an olive with the black mondo grass, *Ophiopogon planiscapus* 'Nigrescens'. Another example is the underplanting of the Judas tree, *Cercis canadensis* 'Forest Pansy', with *Iris* 'Sable', a tall bearded iris.

6. Clothe the walls with climbers. Train wisteria and vines to liven up a plain house wall. In winter, the bare branches add character. Other climbers used here include *Clematis viticella*, *Trachelospermum jasminoides* (star jasmine) and the exuberant blush-white *Rosa* 'Madame Alfred Carrière'.

7. Light up the night. At night this garden is lit up with lanterns and candles – some mounted on the house wall, others dotted about on raised beds and tables.

8. Use succulents as architectural container plants. There are so many varieties to choose from – loose and trailing, spiked and upright, rosette-shaped – and they also come in a variety of greens, reds and a deep purply brown. In warmer areas you can leave succulents out all year round, but some will need shelter in cold, wet winters.

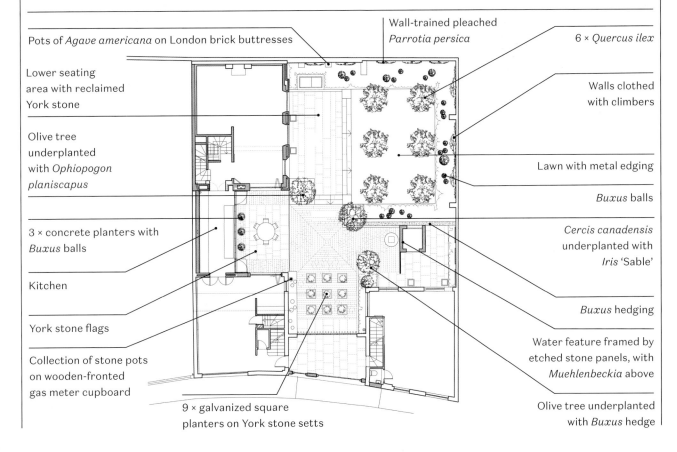

Pots of *Agave americana* on London brick buttresses

Lower seating area with reclaimed York stone

Olive tree underplanted with *Ophiopogon planiscapus*

3 × concrete planters with *Buxus* balls

Kitchen

York stone flags

Collection of stone pots on wooden-fronted gas meter cupboard

9 × galvanized square planters on York stone setts

Wall-trained pleached *Parrotia persica*

6 × *Quercus ilex*

Walls clothed with climbers

Lawn with metal edging

Buxus balls

Cercis canadensis underplanted with *Iris* 'Sable'

Buxus hedging

Water feature framed by etched stone panels, with *Muehlenbeckia* above

Olive tree underplanted with *Buxus* hedge

INTERCONNECTING AREAS

The Details

A row of clipped *Buxus* (box) in concrete planters with *Soleirolia soleirolii* (mind-your-own-business) among the cobbles.

Two tall pots of *Rosmarinus officinalis* Prostratus Group below the wall-trained vine, *Vitis coignetiae*.

Galvanized pots of lavender with blue agapanthus in the raised beds above and below the pots.

Purple oxalis, a fern and succulents in pots above cupboards built to hide unattractive gas meters.

The copper tints of heuchera with spikes of astelia behind a selection of succulents in small pots.

An espaliered *Parrotia persicaria*, also known as Persian ironwood, provides rich autumn colour.

Topiaried *Quercus ilex* (holm oak) on the lawn with *Agave americana* (American aloe) in pots sitting on top of the brick buttresses.

Bright blue agapanthus and purple geraniums under the olive trees in the raised bed.

Neisha Crosland designed the tiles on the wall outside the adjacent studio, with its herringbone brick path.

A Modernist Garden

CHRIS GHYSELEN

A broad double perennial border sits at the heart of this garden. This is a bold modernist scheme, using plants to paint a naturalistic picture. The forms of the grasses and perennials are wild and effervescent, which is in deliberate contrast to the stark geometry of the hedges that frame them. This suburban garden in Flanders measures 1,000sq m (10,800sq ft), but the design feels as open as the skies above, thanks to its simplicity. The horticultural tradition in this part of the country is for growing hedges and shrubs that give form and structure in the low winter light. The design takes this idiom as its starting point. You can see this in the double horizontals of dark yew and the lighter beech hedges. The formality echoes the lines of the modern property and is reflected in the sharp angles of the pool and stepping stones. A path laid with traditional Belgian setts is edged with flowing borders of *Pennisetum*, an ornamental grass, which prepare the viewer for the explosion that is to come. So far all has been restrained, but that changes the moment you enter the rectangle of beech hedging. Purple asters, bold pink persicaria and fiery heleniums are set against sprays of ornamental grasses and soft spires of *Perovskia atriplicifolia* (Russian sage). This is a plant lover's paradise, but one that shouldn't cause its owners too much of a headache. Every plant has been chosen because it does well and lives for a long time. Best of all, these low-maintenance perennials do not need much more than tidying up each autumn.

Left: Asters, persicaria and clump-forming grasses form repeating patterns of colour and form in the large borders. The key to this type of mixed-perennial scheme is to select plants that stay standing in autumn and winter so their silhouettes can create interest.

A MODERNIST GARDEN

Design Checklist

1. Underpin a naturalistic planting with dependable border plants. Key plants here are *Persicaria* 'Red Baron', *P. amplexicaulis* 'Early Pink Lady' and 'Firedance'; *Perovskia* 'Little Spire'; the bergamot, *Monarda* 'Violet Queen'; the coneflower, *Echinacea purpurea* 'Pica Bella'; *Eupatorium maculatum* 'Laag', *Saponaria* × *lempergii* 'Max Frei' and *Aster pyrenaeus* 'Lutetia'.

2. Think about providing winter silhouettes. Cold dry winters are best for sustaining plant stems. If the climate is prone to persistent wet, then stems are more likely to rot. Many perennials provide seedheads that are as beautiful as their blooms.

3. Allow space for your perennial border. A border with interest from summer into autumn featuring large grasses, daisies and other prairie-like plants needs to be deep enough for these 'big hitters' so that they feel airy and their stems can move freely.

4. Use geraniums as border plants, being tough, long-lasting gap-fillers. In the large perennial borders in this garden, Chris Ghyselen has used several, repeating them through the planting to create rhythm (see right). Try *Geranium psilostemon* (American cranesbill) and *G.* 'Ann Folkard', 'Dilys', 'Nimbus' and Patricia.

5. Use hedges to make a modernist statement. Evergreen hedges can be used to provide privacy and divide up areas to create a sense of theatre. You can clip them into different shapes, wave patterns and ellipses. Or create a simple, reductionist, green geometry of cubes or spheres.

6. Create a naturalistic effect using grasses. The key grasses in this border are the tufted hair grass, *Deschampsia cespitosa* 'Goldschleier', *Miscanthus sinensis* 'Morning Light' and *Carex muskingumensis* 'Oehme'.

7. Create rhythm. A modernist border learns from nature by building in repeating patterns that please the eye. You can do this in two ways: firstly by not choosing too many disparate plants and, secondly, by selecting and positioning plants to create repeating waves of colour, or shape or height. Weave a strongly structural plant throughout the border to create unity.

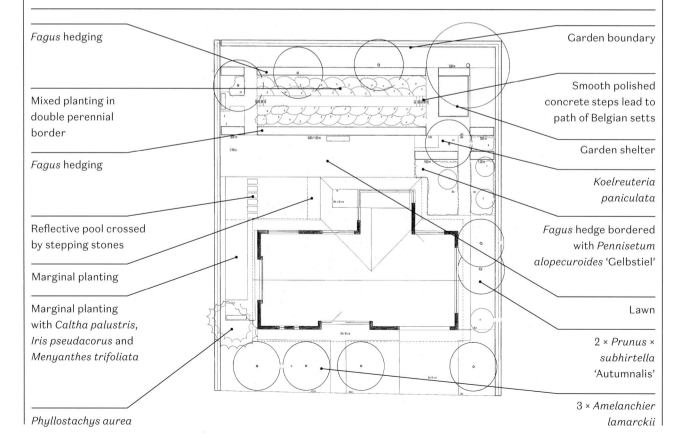

Fagus hedging

Mixed planting in double perennial border

Fagus hedging

Reflective pool crossed by stepping stones

Marginal planting

Marginal planting with *Caltha palustris*, *Iris pseudacorus* and *Menyanthes trifoliata*

Phyllostachys aurea

Garden boundary

Smooth polished concrete steps lead to path of Belgian setts

Garden shelter

Koelreuteria paniculata

Fagus hedge bordered with *Pennisetum alopecuroides* 'Gelbstiel'

Lawn

2 × *Prunus* × *subhirtella* 'Autumnalis'

3 × *Amelanchier lamarckii*

The beech hedge bordered with the ornamental grass *Pennisetum alopecuroides* 'Gelbstiel'.

Smooth polished concrete steps contrast with the Belgian setts.

The design of the garden builds on the tradition in this part of Belgium for growing hedges and shrubs.

Floating rectangular stepping stones reinforce the strong geometry of the pool and hedges.

The drama of the perennial borders is just visible beyond the beech hedge.

The Details

A double hedge of *Pennisetum alopecuroides* 'Gelbstiel'.

The brilliant blue flowers of *Ceratostigma willmottianum* (Chinese plumbago) in the foreground with the tall purple spires of *Perovskia atriplicifolia* (Russian sage) behind.

Sedum, ceratostigma and phlomis to the left of the steps with flaming pink spikes of persicaria on the right.

The naturalistic perennials are the perfect foil for the stark lines of the dark yew hedge and the brick wall.

Where the Wild Things Grow

CHARLOTTE HARRIS

This garden won a Gold medal at the RHS Chelsea Flower Show 2017. The striking design was inspired by the Canadian boreal landscape of pines and larches, and its delicate wetlands. However, the garden doesn't recreate a part of Canada. It was more a case of learning from nature and picking up on its colours, textures and atmosphere. This garden is subtle with a wonderful attention to detail, from the charred larch boardwalk that makes a nod to the regenerative nature of fire to the burnished wall of the copper pavilion. The pavilion was inspired by the hunters' lodges that Charlotte Harris saw as she canoed through the Canadian wilderness. 'They were little more than shacks which had been patched up and were very basic with gaps through the walls or open windows that the vegetation was pushing through. I wanted something that spoke of their presence and which also framed different views of the planting,' she says. The result succeeds in being beautiful, functional and full of tonal richness. As you walk across the floor of sliced granite, the louvres offer a changing view of the planting. The copper also picks up on the orange tones of the cones of *Pinus banksiana* (Jack pine), as well as referring to the mineral wealth of this part of Canada. In contrast to the angular pavilion, granite boulders and muscular trees, the planting is soft. It uses lots of natives from columbines and harebells to grasses and ferns. It's a garden that shows the importance of standing still and observing, of being aware of location and where your garden sits in the landscape.

Left: Delicate marginal plantings, with *Camassia quamash* (common camassia), fringe the path leading across the boardwalk to the pavilion in this celebration of the 150th anniversary of the Confederation of Canada for the RHS Chelsea Flower Show 2017.

WHERE THE WILD THINGS GROW

Design Checklist

1. Celebrate shade. Look at a wood to see how nature responds to the shade beneath trees. Contrasting textures work in dappled light – use ferns and woodland grasses, and light up dark corners with white and pale blue flowers.

2. Allow natural weathering. Let hard materials soften and burnish so they develop character like the copper wall on the pavilion. A wooden table looks more beautiful left silvered and grey rather than varnished each year.

3. Use colour accents. The natural plantings are highlighted by orange–red martagon lilies, *Lilium martagon* 'Arabian Night', acid-yellow *Zizia aurea* (golden alexanders), purple iris and aquilegias, blue *Campanula* (harebell) and rust-red *Geum rivale* (water avens).

4. Choose timber seating. The block seats in the pavilion are carved from timber that was charred and then polished to a smooth, lustrous black finish. Domestic garden options would be using thick slices of tree trunk as stools or making benches from new oak sleepers.

5. Pay attention to detail. Note the attention paid to the edge of the boardwalk. One end has been carved to mirror the curves of the boulder, with just enough space between for pebbles, while the other mirrors the rhomboid forms of the sliced granite floor.

6. Stick with your local vernacular. What are local structures made of? Using local materials not only helps local trades, but also grounds the garden and gives it a heritage and history.

7. Provide a backdrop to planting. The deep purple of *Aquilegia canadensis* (Canadian columbine), the white of *Silene latifolia* (campion) and the soft greens of *Deschampsia cespitosa* (tufted hair grass) and *Onoclea sensibilis* (sensitive fern) are given definition by the grey wall behind.

8. Set the mood with trees and shrubs. The 50-year-old Jack pines and the silver-leaved *Salix exigua* (coyote willow) provide a sense of place. Below is a storey of shrubs and subshrubs that gives the garden its depth. These include *Alnus glutinosa* (common alder), *Viburnum opulus* (guelder rose) and *Myrica gale* (bog myrtle).

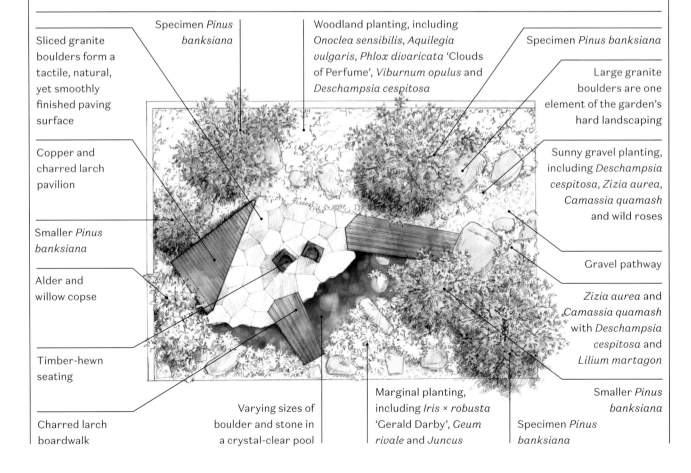

Sliced granite boulders form a tactile, natural, yet smoothly finished paving surface

Copper and charred larch pavilion

Smaller *Pinus banksiana*

Alder and willow copse

Timber-hewn seating

Charred larch boardwalk

Specimen *Pinus banksiana*

Varying sizes of boulder and stone in a crystal-clear pool

Woodland planting, including *Onoclea sensibilis, Aquilegia vulgaris, Phlox divaricata* 'Clouds of Perfume', *Viburnum opulus* and *Deschampsia cespitosa*

Marginal planting, including *Iris × robusta* 'Gerald Darby', *Geum rivale* and *Juncus*

Specimen *Pinus banksiana*

Specimen *Pinus banksiana*

Large granite boulders are one element of the garden's hard landscaping

Sunny gravel planting, including *Deschampsia cespitosa, Zizia aurea, Camassia quamash* and wild roses

Gravel pathway

Zizia aurea and *Camassia quamash* with *Deschampsia cespitosa* and *Lilium martagon*

Smaller *Pinus banksiana*

Soft violet *Iris × robusta* 'Gerald Darby' with the dusty pink flowerheads of *Geum rivale* (water avens).

Pinus banksiana (Jack pine), is native to Canada and fiercely resistant to cold.

As you walk through the pavilion, the copper louvres offer a changing window onto the planting.

The pavilion is surrounded by plantings of deciduous *Onoclea sensibilis* (sensitive fern), native to Canada.

The pavilion of burnished copper has been positioned to catch and reflect the afternoon sun.

WHERE THE WILD THINGS GROW

The Details

Menyanthes trifoliata (bogbean) grows in wet, peaty ground and in shallow water margins. In summer, it produces distinctive white flowers that are tinged with pink.

Boulders interplanted with *Zizia aurea* (golden alexanders) and *Deschampsia cespitosa* (tufted hair grass).

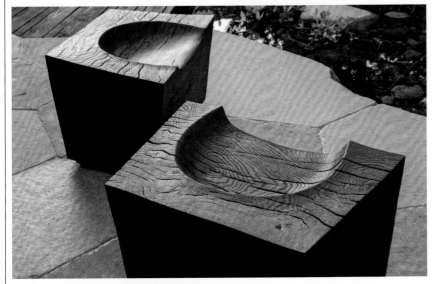

The charred timber seats were made by Jim Partridge and Liz Walmsley.

Often called wild parsley, *Zizia aurea* grows wild in Canada. It copes well with moist ground and partial shade.

5

Other Spaces

Unique by Design

MATT KEIGHTLEY

Settled and serene, this is a garden that draws on subtle details in the architecture and interior of the house, resulting in a space that encourages a desire to explore. The expansive concrete terrace projecting from the rear of the property is far from utilitarian, and the tonal changes in the aggregate create wonderful movement and texture in what is typically perceived as a cold product. Concrete ribs were installed to play with the perspective and draw focus across the width of the garden and towards important elements such as the specimen magnolia and wider landscape. These features are bold and seemingly conceptual but play a crucial role in exaggerating the sense of space. The mature trees in the scheme give the garden structure; gnarled and twisted stems are striking both during the day and when uplit at night. The hard landscape is set out in a 'wishbone' form and paths gradually taper as they glide through the dense planting and stretch views down the length of the garden. Accenting the geometry of the rear elevation to the property, the path pushes to the right of the magnolia, encouraging users to take their time and contemplate their surroundings. Drifts of mostly partial-shade lovers snake through the garden and between the horizontal ribs, softening the angular approach to the hard landscape. The ribs provide shelter and shade in unusual places, facilitating interesting planting combinations, such as ferns in close proximity to tulips. Undulation of the soil level provides movement, depth and layers, creating a scheme that can be enjoyed from all angles. As cooking outdoors is important to the owners, a dedicated space was created at a lower level so it could be practical and big enough without drawing attention away from the planting.

Right: A framed vista providing the elegant and muted interior with an injection of colour, through the bold and verdant greens of the planting palette.

UNIQUE BY DESIGN

Design Checklist

1. Consider a concrete terrace. Large terraces are perfect for minimalist gardens and can be created with few or no joint lines at all. To avoid a terrace becoming too imposing, the interface details are crucial. Add shadow gaps or underplanting to make the terrace feel less heavy.

2. Plan a barbecue area like any terrace. I love cooking outdoors so I get excited when clients request space for this. Cooking spaces should be large enough for both socializing and cooking.

3. Transform your garden, provide it with maturity and make it feel complete with specimen trees. Multistemmed forms look architecturally striking, both during the day and lit up at night. As the tree develops, prune in a way that suits you and your garden – an umbrella form can offer shade as well as framing views.

4. Soften boundary walls with frame-grown climbers. These temper harsh edges and, by doing so, draw in the wider landscape, so making your garden feel bigger. The advantage of using frames is that they provide the perfect support for growing other plants through them. For example, start with jasmine and encourage roses through, or start with ivy and encourage hydrangeas through.

5. Ensure the best use of space and increase the ways in which you can use your garden with multiple seating areas. If there isn't seating for lounging, dining or reading at the end of your garden, you have less reason to go there.

6. Consider the synergy between interior and exterior spaces. Subtle accents pulled out into the garden through colour or design details and, of course, overall styling will make the garden feel like an extra room, especially in smaller spaces.

7. Choose plants with interesting foliage for effective planting structure. You don't need specimen topiary or shrubs, as herbaceous structure can be just as dramatic and exciting. Contrasting leaf shape and texture options are endless.

8. Accessorize to personalise your garden. Add furniture to suit the style, pots to layer the planting, and lanterns to create atmosphere at night. Artwork and sculpture can also put the finishing touches to an outdoor living space.

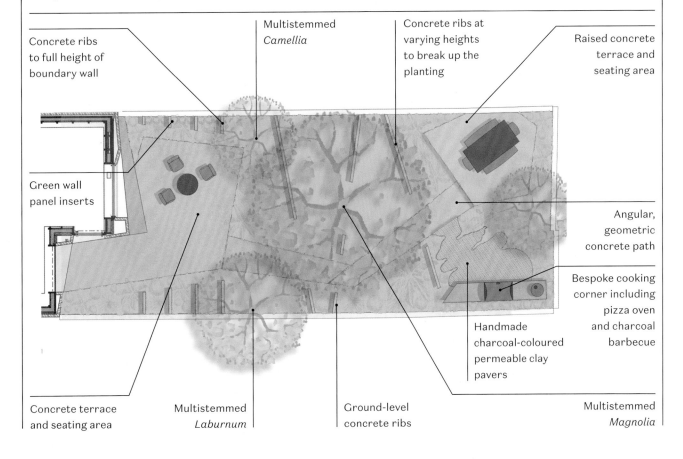

Concrete ribs to full height of boundary wall

Multistemmed *Camellia*

Concrete ribs at varying heights to break up the planting

Raised concrete terrace and seating area

Green wall panel inserts

Angular, geometric concrete path

Bespoke cooking corner including pizza oven and charcoal barbecue

Handmade charcoal-coloured permeable clay pavers

Concrete terrace and seating area

Multistemmed *Laburnum*

Ground-level concrete ribs

Multistemmed *Magnolia*

Bespoke vertical concrete ribs
divide the green wall, adding
interest and also complementing
a similar internal detail.

The contemporary picnic bench is enveloped by planting
on a concrete terrace that seems to float, thanks to the
shadow-gap detail over the intersecting path.

The Details

The concrete ribs in the border dissect
the planting, encouraging the eye
across the width of the garden.

A sunken cooking space sits neatly in the back corner of the
garden. The bespoke work surface provides ample cooking
space, while the level ensures it is as discreet as possible.

An angular geometric path tapers to
elongate the feeling of space as it cuts
through the garden.

CASE STUDY

A Dark and Narrow Garden

SUE TOWNSEND

Two mature lime trees and months of building work on the period house had made this dark, narrow side garden dry and unprepossessing. Builders had left the soil badly compacted and there was a complete lack of privacy as the garden faced directly onto the pavement. The award-winning designer Sue Townsend has transformed the area, creating a quiet green spot that invites you to sit outside, hidden from passers-by by a tall, handsome pleached *Carpinus* (hornbeam) screen. A sinuous gravel path flows along the length of the garden and is softened by new raised beds on either side, which are planted with perennials. The curves slow the visitor down, while the rich planting in a palette of blues, purples, pink and lime-green encourages you to stop and look – all of which has the desired effect of making the garden seem bigger and much greener. Seating areas have been placed at each end of the path where they catch the morning and afternoon sun. There is a breakfast area on a raised stone terrace outside the kitchen, and at the other end is a large circular terrace for lunch and supper. The bike and bin sheds were painted black and softened with a green living roof. The new planting beds were filled with fresh topsoil and edged with rusted Corten steel, which looks contemporary while also working with the period building. Counterintuitively, the more plants, the greater the impression of space, so the luxuriant planting by the house and in front of the hedge gives a dense woodland feel.

Left: A sinuous gravel path allows rainwater to reach the lime trees, while a rich palette of plants gives year-round interest. Spring bulbs start the season with *Tulipa* 'White Triumphator' and glossy, deep purple 'Queen of Night'.

A DARK AND NARROW GARDEN

Design Checklist

1. Give your garden a sense of age. Opt for reclaimed stone, such as York stone, which has inherent variations. Use natural timber and allow this to weather (rather than varnishing it). Leave a trellis unvarnished, plant it with climbers and it will fade to an attractive silvery colour.

2. Make the garden seem bigger by packing in the plants. Another trick is to use plants with lots of detail to catch the eye and keep it in the garden rather than drifting towards the boundary.

3. Erect a living screen for privacy. The *Carpinus* (hornbeam) hedge on the boundary is made by tying branches to horizontal wires supported by posts. Buy ready-trained plants, if possible, or train your own. To create a screen, simply plant close together. Once mature, prune the plants in winter.

4. Make a feature of storage with a green roof. The storage cupboards for bikes and bins were painted black, then given a living green roof. These can be planted on virtually flat or sloping roofs, though they need to be suitably weight-bearing to support the soil. Specialist companies can install or deliver rolls of turf that are preplanted, often with meadow plants or sedums.

5. Make the path curve. In a small garden such as this, introduce a sinuous path so it takes longer to walk through the space. This has the advantage of encouraging a feeling of relaxation.

6. Manage dry ground. Typical of a city garden with mature trees, the soil in this plot is particularly dry. To improve matters, install irrigation systems of leaky hoses through planting beds. Here, loose gravel was used on the paths so rainwater can reach the tree roots.

7. Chase the sun. This is particularly important in a small, shady side garden, which only receives sunlight at certain times of the day. In this case, the two sitting areas were sited at opposite ends of the path to catch the morning breakfast sun and light at the end of the afternoon.

8. Practical can be beautiful. Metal railings, 90cm (3ft) high, were installed to stop anyone falling into the deep light-well. Choosing the right style to match the period of the house was essential, while painting them the same colour added a nice finishing touch.

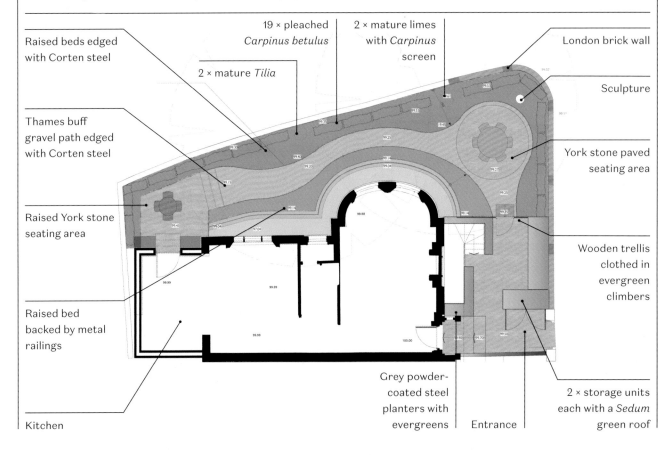

Raised beds edged with Corten steel

2 × mature *Tilia*

19 × pleached *Carpinus betulus*

2 × mature limes with *Carpinus* screen

London brick wall

Sculpture

Thames buff gravel path edged with Corten steel

York stone paved seating area

Raised York stone seating area

Wooden trellis clothed in evergreen climbers

Raised bed backed by metal railings

Kitchen

Grey powder-coated steel planters with evergreens

Entrance

2 × storage units each with a *Sedum* green roof

The loose Thames buff gravel
path edged with Corten steel.

Black-painted storage sheds for bikes
and bins topped with a green living roof.

Woodland plantings of *Dryopteris
affinis* 'Cristata' and purple
Aquilegia vulgaris (columbine).

The pleached *Carpinus* (hornbeam)
hedge screens the seating area
from the street.

The Details

The pleached *Carpinus* (hornbeam) screen
is trained on horizontal wires fixed to posts.

The two mature limes with the *Carpinus*
(hornbeam) screen.

A layer of loose mulch helps to
trap moisture beneath the mature
lime trees.

CASE STUDY

Year-round Good Looks

JAMES ALDRIDGE

Broad white limestone steps lead the eye out of the modern interior and across the sunken terrace up to the lawn, which conceals a room for the clients' children. Green spheres of *Buxus* (box) cluster against the back wall, grounding the design and providing a contrast with the gentle tracery of *Nothofagus antarctica* (Antarctic beech) behind. This is a design that employs great sleight of hand to carve out a garden from a typically small space in central London. The scheme starts from the moment you open the front gate and cross the threshold. A path of reclaimed York stone leads to the front steps, with side paths of pale Portland limestone chippings. In front of the house is a mass planting of cloud-clipped box that conceals the lower terrace area. Left of the path the verticals of the *Pyrus* (pear) trees contrast with large random 'beehive' and ball-shaped box. These are interplanted with *Libertia*, *Cyrtomium*, *Anenome × hybrida* 'Honorine Jobert', *Helleborus*, *Leucojum* and white camassias. Already we see the key palette is going to be green, off-white and dark greys. As the narrow side path turns the corner, the eye picks up the neat echo of the right angles formed by the white walls of the minimalist house. This formality is softened with plantings of a multistemmed *Ginkgo*, *Pyrus calleryana* 'Chanticleer', *Agapanthus africanus* 'Albus', *Iris confusa*, *Hydrangea seemannii*, *Cyrtomium falcatum* (Japanese holly fern) and *Trachelospermum jasminoides* (star jasmine).

Right: The lawn sits above a children's nook, hence the inset skylight. In the corner by the steps, a number of box balls tie in the design of the lower terrace to that of the upper level. There is a pleasing symmetry in the horizontal lines of the wall-trained hornbeam with those of the simple dark grey railing.

YEAR-ROUND GOOD LOOKS

Design Checklist

1. Give your garden a green backbone. This is crucial to the design of this garden and works with the hard landscaping to provide two- and three-dimensional structure. The freestanding espalier-trained *Carpinus* (hornbeam) is green in spring and summer, then turns a rich deep copper in autumn. It keeps these colourful leaves almost until the new buds break.

2. Keep it simple. There's no need for fiddly bobbles and finials in this design. The metal railings are not designed to draw unnecessary attention. Their clean lines match those of the pleached hornbeam and the simplicity of the modern-build house.

3. Box clever. Evergreen clipped box looks good all year round and is relatively simple to keep neat and tidy. The mass planting of cloud-pruned *Buxus* (box) in front of the house needs to be hand-clipped annually. Either buy ready-grown box balls or, to save money, buy young plants and train them yourself.

4. Let the interior inform the exterior. Echoing the pale kitchen, limestone steps link with the simple limestone chipping paths at the front and side of the house. To keep the same crisp lines, borders and lawns are confined with galvanized steel edges.

5. Think about where you are going to spend time. Standing by a kitchen sink is hard to avoid, so create a beautiful view. Here, the creamy white sprays of evergreen *Libertia grandiflora* are succeeded in autumn by attractive seed pods.

6. Use the space. Beneath the lawn there is a hidden room, the children's nook. The skylight lets light into this secret space.

7. Limit the number of plants. Just pick a few and make them work, repeating form and colours across the space. Think about leaf shapes, too, contrasting delicate and airy acers, for example, with strong, strappy *Agapanthus africanus* 'Albus' and the small, precise foliage of box.

8. Choose sculptural seating. The bespoke iroko wood dining table and seating in this garden perfectly echo the neat, straight lines of the hard landscaping.

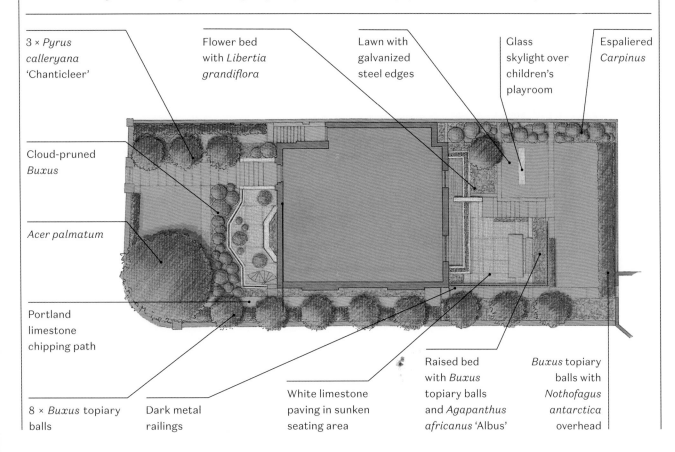

3 × *Pyrus calleryana* 'Chanticleer'

Flower bed with *Libertia grandiflora*

Lawn with galvanized steel edges

Glass skylight over children's playroom

Espaliered *Carpinus*

Cloud-pruned *Buxus*

Acer palmatum

Portland limestone chipping path

8 × *Buxus* topiary balls

Dark metal railings

White limestone paving in sunken seating area

Raised bed with *Buxus* topiary balls and *Agapanthus africanus* 'Albus'

Buxus topiary balls with *Nothofagus antarctica* overhead

YEAR-ROUND GOOD LOOKS

The Details

The exquisitely trained *Carpinus* (hornbeam) screen with globes of *Buxus* (box).

A mainly green border of *Libertia grandiflora* and *Cyrtomium falcatum* (Japanese holly fern).

The lawn is planted with a single *Acer palmatum* and surrounded by a hedge of *Prunus lusitanica* (Portugal laurel), which has reached a height of 3m (10ft). Behind are three *Pyrus calleryana* 'Chanticleer'.

Heavy panicles of the dramatic white *Wisteria floribunda* 'Alba', a variety of Japanese wisteria.

The view from the kitchen through uprights of creamy *Libertia grandiflora*.

The cool white geometry of the Portland limestone chipping paths echoes that of the house.

The lines of the dining table and stools sit harmoniously on the subtle surface finish of the limestone terrace.

CASE STUDY

A Shady Courtyard

STUART CRAINE

The transformation of this shady back garden is a remarkable achievement. When Stuart Craine first saw the plot, it was still a building site after a major refurbishment of the house. There was no soil, just London clay, and the plot was also overlooked on three sides. Running the floor seamlessly from inside to outdoors gives a sense of increased space, while the floor-to-ceiling window folds away to allow as much space as possible in this courtyard that measures only 31sq m (334sq ft). The London stock brick walls were in good condition, so the same material was used to create the raised beds into which is cantilevered an iroko bench. Slatted screens, also in the same iroko hardwood, were erected on top of the walls to provide privacy, as well as to hide the air conditioning unit. Using the minimum of materials helps make the space seem more generous, as does keeping the planting palette to mainly green. Jasmine fills the garden with its scent on summer evenings, while roses and camellias provide spots of white and palest pink to help lighten the shade. Planting the walls increases the verdancy, as does the woodland underplanting of ferns and *Liriope* that now frames the centrepiece: the rusted steel sculpture by Max Woodruff. At night the garden comes into its own, creating a view from the dining table as well as somewhere to sit outside. As you look down on the garden from the living sedum roof on the first floor, it now looks fresh, green and inviting.

Right: A cantilevered iroko hardwood bench invites you into the courtyard, which flows seamlessly from the house. At the centre of the garden, and uplit at night, stands a rusted Corten steel sculpture by Max Woodruff. This garden is a wonderful example of how much can be achieved in a small space.

A SHADY COURTYARD

Design Checklist

1. Plant for months of colour. Stuart Craine chose shrubs for interest from late winter to late autumn. Evergreen, variegated and scented pink *Daphne odora* 'Aureomarginata' (late winter to mid-spring) is followed by white-flowered *Camellia japonica* 'Madame Henri Cormerais' (early to late spring), while *Rosa* 'New Dawn' is in bloom from early summer to the end of autumn.

2. Underplant in small areas if you want to use all the available planting space to give a woodland feel. The plants used here do well in the dry shade typical of terraced city gardens. They include two ferns, *Polystichum setiferum* 'Plumoso-Divisilobum' and *P. polyblepharum* (Japanese lace fern), and *Liriope muscari*.

3. Screen from neighbours. This garden is overlooked on three sides, so the simplest screening builds up the existing London stock brick walls with slatted iroko horizontal fence panels.

4. Use the space. Every inch counts in a small garden. The cantilevered bench does this brilliantly. The seat and iroko hardwood fence are left unvarnished so they will weather to a soft silvery grey.

5. Make use of verticals to double the green by planting up walls and fences. *Trachelospermum jasminoides* (star jasmine) is popular as it has evergreen foliage that turns bronze in autumn and white flowers that are heavily scented.

6. Introduce structure with clipped evergreens. Here, the dark evergreen needles of *Taxus baccata* (common yew) are trimmed into spheres that repeat through the planting to give year-round structure and unity.

7. Unify planting by restricting your colour palette. The green palette with accents of white and pink unifies this garden. The perennials *Astrantia* 'Buckland' and *Aquilegia vulgaris* 'William Guinness' both add summer interest. The purple and white aquilegia flowers in late spring and early summer, while the astrantia continues the show from early into late summer. The purple liriope keeps going until late autumn.

8. Use a sculpture as a focal point. The height and scale of the weathered Corten steel Max Woodruff sculpture make the courtyard seem larger, while its minimalism sits well with the contemporary feel of the space.

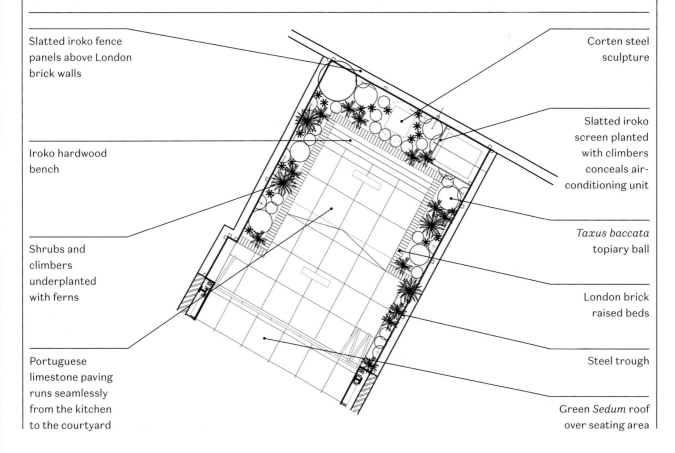

Slatted iroko fence panels above London brick walls

Iroko hardwood bench

Shrubs and climbers underplanted with ferns

Portuguese limestone paving runs seamlessly from the kitchen to the courtyard

Corten steel sculpture

Slatted iroko screen planted with climbers conceals air-conditioning unit

Taxus baccata topiary ball

London brick raised beds

Steel trough

Green *Sedum* roof over seating area

A SHADY COURTYARD

The
Details

In the right-hand raised bed are ferns,
a yew sphere and *Liriope muscari*.

The left-hand raised bed is planted
with *Camellia japonica* 'Madame Henri
Cormerais' in the far corner, as well as
Daphne odora 'Aureomarginata' and a
sphere of *Taxus baccata* (common yew).

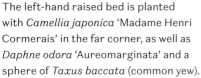

Trachelospermum jasminoides
(star jasmine) grows in a tall trough
underplanted with *Liriope muscari*.

Trachelospermum jasminoides (star jasmine) and the pale pink repeating blooms of the climbing rose 'New Dawn'.

The view from the kitchen demonstrates that the Corten steel sculpture by Max Woodruff is at the centre of the design.

Polystichum polyblepharum (Japanese lace fern), *Liriope muscari* and *Astrantia* 'Buckland' provide a green plinth for the Max Woodruff sculpture.

CASE STUDY

A City Roof Terrace

ANDREW WILSON & GAVIN MCWILLIAM

This contemporary city roof garden has won a slew of awards for its bold and innovative design. It manages to settle with natural ease in the city roofscape of chimney pots and roof tiles, while at the same time brimming with textured plantings reminiscent of the English countryside. There are three levels in all, each of which has been given a distinct yet interrelated design. The dining area is on the lowest level. Glass balustrades lead up steps to the middle terrace. This was designed for entertaining and has a chic urban finish with a rendered fireplace and smooth basalt floor that shines when wet. The boundary is given definition with a rusted Corten steel screen that has been laser-cut in Morse code to allow the light (and geraniums) to play through the holes. The same rusted steel has been used for the large tree planters, and its warm hues pick up on nearby terracotta chimney pots. The planting is an abstraction of an English hedgerow with pleached *Acer campestre* (field maple) providing privacy. These and the multistemmed *Crataegus* (hawthorn) are underplanted with perennials and grasses. At night, uplighting below the multistemmed trees bounces off the leaf canopy, creating a diffuse effect. The wooden deck on the top level is a suntrap with city views. A box hedge, also in rusted steel planters, provides shelter from the prevailing wind. To finish, there is a living roof that is partly planted with a low sedum mat to contrast with three drifts of mixed perennials that include grasses, herbs and flowering plants, chosen because they can cope with the exposed site.

Left: The middle terrace has a basalt floor that echoes the smooth rendering on the contemporary fireplace. Rusted Corten steel was used for the planters and screen. The planting is a subtle take on the traditional English hedgerow.

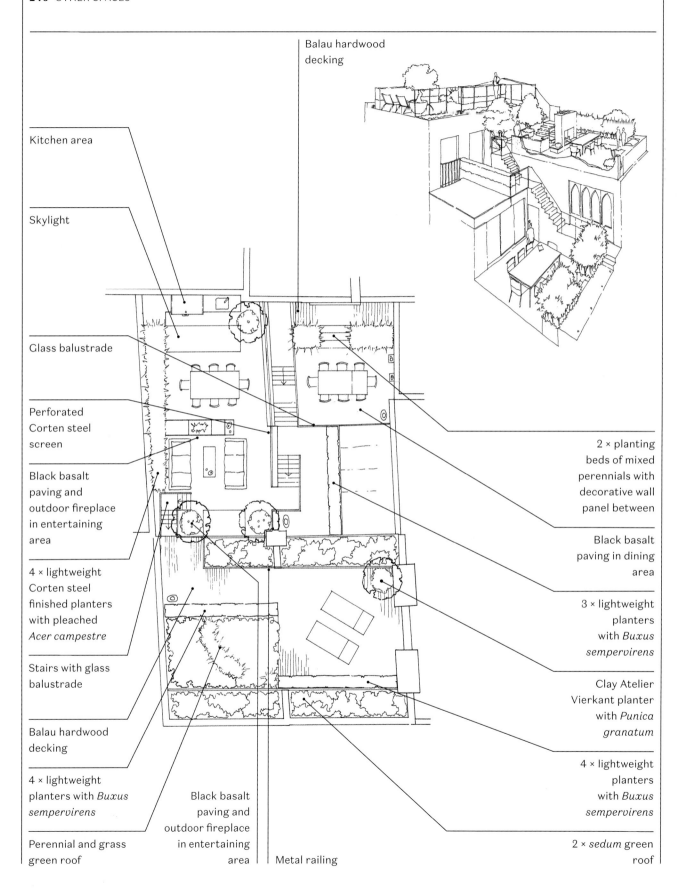

Balau hardwood decking

Kitchen area

Skylight

Glass balustrade

Perforated Corten steel screen

Black basalt paving and outdoor fireplace in entertaining area

4 × lightweight Corten steel finished planters with pleached *Acer campestre*

Stairs with glass balustrade

Balau hardwood decking

4 × lightweight planters with *Buxus sempervirens*

Perennial and grass green roof

Black basalt paving and outdoor fireplace in entertaining area

Metal railing

2 × planting beds of mixed perennials with decorative wall panel between

Black basalt paving in dining area

3 × lightweight planters with *Buxus sempervirens*

Clay Atelier Vierkant planter with *Punica granatum*

4 × lightweight planters with *Buxus sempervirens*

2 × *sedum* green roof

A CITY ROOF TERRACE

Design Checklist

1. Consider weight-bearing issues.
It is essential when making any type of roof terrace that the structure is strong enough to support all the hard and soft landscaping and, most importantly, that it can sustain the weight of saturated soil. To be safe, it is best to consult a structural engineer.

2. Install a green roof. These can be 'extensive', with a planting depth of 5–15cm (2–6in), or intensive, with more than 30cm (12in) of growing medium. Both systems were used in this garden.

The extensive roof used a mat of *Lindum sedumplus* and the intensive area a Diadem 150 system planted with a sweep of *Lavandula* × *intermedia* 'Gros Bleu' between a mix of perennials and grasses.

3. Opt for a skylight. Details like this can make or break a design; seek expert advice so that the job is done properly. The one in this garden was designed and installed by 23 Architecture.

4. Plant trees that can cope with the exposed and windy conditions of a roof terrace. Ensure that they are watered regularly and feed them when required.

5. Animate the space. The Corten steel screen plays with light and shadow. The holes were cut using a CAD file that was created by the design team and lists in Morse code the names of everyone involved in the project. The screen was secured by bolting it onto a structural beam below the paving.

6. Choose decking material with care. The decking here was made with balau, a tightly grained tropical hardwood that is hard-wearing and also knot-free. This wood is relatively slip-free and comes in a range of colours, but it is best left unvarnished so that it can weather to a lovely soft grey.

7. Provide adequate drainage. The paving and decking were installed on adjustable paving pads above the drainage system. This consists of a finished surface that is level with the roof and is laid to fall, thereby allowing free drainage.

8. Uplight from below trees to create a soft and diffuse effect as the light bounces off the leaves. Both sides of the fireplace were uplit, while LED lighting was placed below the wooden sun deck so that it shines up and backlights the sculpture at night. Downlighting on the walls lights the steps for safety.

A hedge of clipped *Buxus* (box) planted in one of the three beds of rusted Corten steel.

The extensive living roof, left, is planted with sedums, while the intensive roof, right, has wavy drifts of mixed perennials and *Lavandula* × *intermedia* 'Gros Bleu'.

Six weathered Corten steel screens were laser-cut with an unusual Morse code pattern. This spells out the names of those involved in the project.

Multistemmed *Crataegus* (hawthorn) underplanted with *Geranium* Rozanne.

A CITY ROOF TERRACE

The Details

A gnarled old pomegranate in a contemporary clay planter from Atelier Vierkant.

Looking from the upper terrace and over the striking containerised plantings of *Crataegus* (hawthorn) on the middle terrace.

The *Geranium* Rozanne growing through the Corten steel panel softens the effect and gives the impression of nature reclaiming hard landscaping.

Geranium Rozanne and *Hakonechloa macra* (Japanese forest grass) in a rusted steel planter from Urbis Design.

Sourcebook

FEATURED DESIGNERS

James Aldridge (p232)
jamesaldridgedesign.com

James Basson (p158)
scapedesign.com

Peter Berg (p44)
gartenlandschaft.com

Christopher Bradley-Hole (p38)
bhsla.co.uk

Jane Brockbank (pp84, 90 & 180)
janebrockbank.com

Declan Buckley (p174)
buckleydesignassociates.com

Stuart Craine (p238)
stuartcraine.com

Chris Ghyselen & Dominique Eeman
(pp50 & 204)
chrisghyselen.be

Charlotte Harris (p210)
harrisbugg.com

Matt Keightley (pp18, 64, 110, 124,
166 & 218)
rosebanklandscaping.co.uk

Sara Jane Rothwell (pp56, 96 & 144)
londongardendesigner.com

Charlotte Rowe (pp26, 78 & 138)
charlotterowe.com

Tom Stuart-Smith (p192)
tomstuartsmith.co.uk

Jo Thompson (p102)
jothompson-garden-design.co.uk

Sue Townsend (p226)
suetownsendgardendesign.co.uk

Sean Walter (pp72, 150, 186 & 198)
theplantspecialist.co.uk

Jo Willems & Jan van Opstal (p132)
heerenhof.com
Check on the website for information
about visiting the garden.

Andrew Wilson & Gavin McWilliam
(pp11 & 244)
mcwilliamstudio.com

Tony Woods (p32)
gardenclublondon.co.uk

HARD LANDSCAPING

Artificial grass
easilawn.com
artificiallawn.co.uk

Bespoke metal
archimetdesigns.co.uk

Bespoke planters
bspokedesign.co.uk

Charred timber cladding
shousugiban.co.uk

Corten steel
starkandgreensmith.com

Instant ivy hedge kits
green-tech.co.uk

Natural swimming ponds
naturalswimmingpools.com

Professional lawn and path edging
cedstone.co.uk

Steel windows
crittall-windows.co.uk

Stone paving and products
londonstone.co.uk

Stone setts
cedstone.co.uk

Timber fence panels
silvatimber.co.uk

ARCHITECTS

23 Architecture
318.studio

LIGHTING

John Cullen
johncullenlighting.com

FURNITURE

Bespoke outdoor fires and firepits
bd-designs.co.uk

Catcastle grey sandstone
dunhouse.co.uk

Contemporary furniture and firepits
encompassco.com
anothercountry.com

Furniture and functional woodwork
jplw.co.uk

Modular outdoor seating
maisonsdumonde.com

Vintage decorative garden reclamation
vintagegardenco.com

Wide range of outdoor furniture
indian-ocean.co.uk

Wooden garden furniture
gazeburvill.com

POTS

Contemporary clay planters
ateliervierkant.com

Contemporary pots and planters
urbisdesign.co.uk

PLAYHOUSES

The Children's Cottage Company
play-houses.com

SCULPTURE

Tom Price
tom-price.com

Max Woodruff
maxwoodruff.co.uk

PLANTS

Bearded iris
www.iris-cayeux.com

Living roofs
enviromat.co.uk

Pleached hedging
ornamental-trees.co.uk
hedgesdirect.co.uk
best4hedging.co.uk

Topiary
hortusloci.co.uk

Trees
deepdale-trees.co.uk

Index

Acknowledgements

I would like to thank:

The RHS and all members involved in the process, for showing their confidence in me as a designer and patience in me as a writer.
Rae Spencer-Jones especially, for holding my hand and holding in there throughout!
Chris Young for his reassuring nods at the right times.
Octopus Publishing Group and all members involved, for their enthusiasm from the beginning and very wise and experienced words of wisdom and advice throughout.
Alison Starling for her pushes/shoves in the right direction, no matter where she was or what she was doing. Her enthusiasm made me believe in the book from the start.
Leanne Bryan for getting us over the finish line with as much gusto as Alison.
Juliette Norsworthy for her seemingly effortless approach to the layout of the entire book and bringing designer Ben Brannan into the project with such elegant results.
Caroline West for going through the book line by line to ensure my grammar didn't spoil the day.
Joanna Chisholm for curating the annotations for the garden plans.
Marianne Majerus for her immeasurable talent, eye for a shot and, of course, vast photo library that made this book possible. I am very fortunate to enjoy her company on a professional and friendship level outside of *RHS Design Outdoors*.
Bennet Smith for his initial edits and rapid-fire responses.
Tiffany Daneff for stepping up and doing something I could not. Taking on the task was a huge ask at that moment in time and I cannot thank her enough.
Rosebank Landscaping and all the lovely people in our company for their support.
Cameron Wilson my pal and bizzo partner for the support and encouragement, regardless of his knowledge about my articulating ability.

To all my family, friends and peers who have been there with me from the start and joined our team on the journey; without them I would not have got to this point.
Matt Keightley

The Publisher would like to thank the garden designers featured for providing information and garden plans for the book, and the garden owners for allowing their gardens to be photographed.

I would like to dedicate this book to my three beautiful girls. Without the relentless and unwavering love, support and encouragement of Katharine, Poppy and Sophie, this, another exciting first in my career, would not have been possible.

Matt Keightley

First published in Great Britain in 2019 by Mitchell Beazley, an imprint of Octopus Publishing Group Ltd,
Carmelite House
50 Victoria Embankment
London EC4Y 0DZ
www.octopusbooks.co.uk

An Hachette UK Company
www.hachette.co.uk

Published by Mitchell Beazley, an imprint of Octopus Publishing Group, in association with the Royal Horticultural Society.

ISBN: 978-1-78472-480-1

A CIP record for this book is available from the British Library.

Printed and bound in China.

FSC
www.fsc.org
MIX
Paper | Supporting responsible forestry
FSC® C008047

10 9 8 7 6 5 4

Photographer Marianne Majerus
RHS Publisher Rae Spencer-Jones
RHS Editors Tim Berry & Simona Hill
Contributing Editor Tiffany Daneff
Designer Ben Brannan
Copy-editor Caroline West

Publisher Alison Starling
Senior Editor Leanne Bryan
Assistant Editor Emily Brickell
Art Director Juliette Norsworthy
Senior Production Manager Katherine Hockley

About the author

Matt Keightley is an award-winning garden designer with more than 12 years' experience in the landscaping industry and a reputation as one of the UK's most exciting young garden designers.

He made waves within the landscaping industry in 2014 when, as a debutant at the RHS Chelsea Flower Show, he was awarded the RHS Silver-Gilt Medal and the highly acclaimed BBC People's Choice Award for his 'Help for Heroes' show garden, dedicated to the wounded men and women of the armed forces. One year later he was back at Chelsea, this time working with Prince Harry for his charity Sentebale. Matt's 'Hope in Vulnerability' show garden earned him another Silver-Gilt medal and the BBC People's Choice Award for the second year running. In 2017, he was appointed to design an RHS/BBC Radio 2 garden for Chelsea with presenter Jeremy Vine. A contemporary space designed around the sense of touch, this immersive, tactile garden featured bold geometric forms juxtaposed with a soft, elegant planting palette. In 2018 he returned to Chelsea with his RHS 'Feel Good Garden' and is now designing a health and wellbeing-themed garden for RHS Garden Wisley.

Matt is now working on projects in the UK and Germany. His personable character and extensive horticultural knowledge ensure that he is a regular guest presenter and speaker at various garden design events and seminars.
www.rosebanklandscaping.co.uk

About the photographer

Marianne Majerus is one of the world's finest garden photographers. Born in Luxembourg and based in London, she is a regular contributor to many international publications, including *House & Garden*, *Gardens Illustrated*, RHS *The Garden* and *The Wall Street Journal*. She has illustrated in excess of 50 books, including, for Mitchell Beazley, *RHS The Urban Gardener* and *Garden Design: A Book of Ideas*. Marianne has won numerous awards for her work, including International Garden Photographer of the Year 2010 and Garden Media Guild Features Photographer of the Year 2013.
www.mariannemajerus.com

About the RHS

The Royal Horticultural Society is the UK's largest gardening charity, dedicated to advancing horticulture and promoting good gardening. Its charitable work includes providing expert advice and information, training the next generation of gardeners and promoting the ecological, aesthetic and psychological benefits of gardening in an urban environment.
www.rhs.org.uk